Steam in Action
Bulleid Pacifics

Steam in Action
Bulleid Pacifics

John Sagar

IAN ALLAN Publishing

First published 1992

ISBN 0 7110 2057 4

© Ian Allan Ltd 1992

Published by Ian Allan Ltd, Shepperton, Surrey;
and printed by Ian Allan Printing Ltd at their
works at Coombelands in Runnymede,
England.

A catalogue record for this book
is available from the British Library.

ACKNOWLEDGEMENTS

In addition to my three fellow contribu-
tors, I should like to thank the following for their invaluable assistance in the
preparation of this book. John Adams
and Richard Greenwood of the Keigh-
ley & Worth Valley Railway for their
down-to-earth approach to the Bulleid
Pacifics and their technical expertise:
Dr John Coiley, Philip Atkins and
Michael Blakemore of the National Railway Museum for guiding me through
their extensive Southern archives: Dick
Riley, who gave me ready access to his
superb photographic collection and
copious records: Dr Graham Ruddock
for information about the preserved
locomotives: and, not least, David Ward
of British Rail, who enabled me to
experience what a Bulleid Pacific in
action really feels like! My thanks are
also due to Lena Covemacker, who
typed the manuscript and became a
Bulleid convert in the process.

DEDICATION
*For all those who are working so
hard to keep the Bulleid Pacifics
alive and kicking.*

Title page:
**Arrangement of nameplate, plaque and
scroll on a modified 'West Country'. The
driving wheels also carry balance weights.**
NRM

Previous page:
**Unmodified 'Battle of Britain' Pacific
No 34066 *Spitfire* provides a superb
evocation of Bulleid's work as it climbs the
Slade Valley out of Ilfracombe with the up
'Atlantic Coast Express' on a beautiful
spring day. *Ian Allan Library***

Right:
**A sharp contrast in styles between
Nos 34033 *Chard* and 7823 *Hook Norton
Manor* at Laira shed, Plymouth on 15 July
1956. *R. C. Riley***

Contents

Front cover:
'Battle of Britain' class 4-6-2 No 34069 *Hawkinge* pauses for water at Yeovil Junction on
22 July 1958 with a westbound freight. This was one of 50 locomotives not to be rebuilt. *R.
C. Riley*

Rear cover, top:
On 23 May 1959, No 34085 *501 Squadron* accelerates the up 'Golden Arrow' away from
Dover past 'D1' 4-4-0 No 31505. *R. C. Riley*

Rear cover, bottom:
The first 'West Country' to be modified was No 34005 *Barnstaple*, seen here hurrying the
down 'Man of Kent' through Chislehurst on 16 May 1959. *R. C. Riley*

ntroduction

At the publisher's behest, the key word in this book is 'action' and there are perhaps no steam locomotives better equipped to illustrate it than the Bulleid Pacifics. Having been born too late, and in too northerly climes, to know them properly in their prime, I first became involved with these locomotives some 10 years ago. Until then, I had never appreciated fully the immense affection and esteem in which they were, and indeed still are, held.

Like some other locomotive classes one can think of, the Bulleids always seem to have attracted star billing. There are probably numerous reasons for this. Their appearance: their distinctive exhaust beat and whistle: the aura of power surrounding them and their capacity for fast running and hill climbing: evocative names accompanied by eye-catching plaques and scrolls: volcanic departures from London termini for Continental destinations: the prestigious trains they frequently worked: the bond which was formed with the men who drove, fired and maintained them:

their ability to whisk people away from the cares of everyday life and deposit them in some remote spot on the Atlantic seaboard for refreshing summer holidays.

Yet, as any tabloid newspaper editor will tell you, the real 'star' combines brilliance with occasional foibles. Perhaps this is one of the keys to understanding the enduring appeal of Bulleid's Pacifics: steam locomotives with a human dimension, an idiosyncratic expression of their designer's ideas and personality. After all, you never hear railway people talk about 'Hawksworths' or 'Thompsons'.

In an attempt to capture the flavour of working with and riding behind the

Below:
A Bulleid Pacific in its pomp. Running at over 80mph, No 35009 *Shaw Savill* whips its 13-coach Plymouth-Waterloo express round a bend six miles south west of Salisbury on the golden evening of 25 September 1954. *G. F. Heiron*

Pacifics, I have tried to include as wide a range of illustrations, covering as many locomotives, as possible. If a few of these have been seen before, I apologise, but feel they are worth seeing again! Observant readers will note that there is a slight bias towards the light Pacifics, because the bulk of recent published material has tended to focus on the 'Merchant Navy' class. I have also drawn on the assistance of three friends and recognised experts in their fields: Dick Hardy, for his knowledge of what it was like to run a railway with these locomotives: Bert Hooker, whose name has become synonymous with extracting high performance from them: and Tony Davies, who has ridden many thousands of miles behind the Bulleid Pacifics, sometimes, as we shall see, along unexpected byways. If the book succeeds in its aims, it will be in no small measure thanks to their efforts.

John Sagar
Bury
November 1991

Chapter One

THE BULLEID PACIFICS — HISTORY AND DEVELOPMENT

The unveiling of the pioneer Bulleid Pacific at Eastleigh in February 1941 must rank with the first appearance on the scene of Gresley's 'A4' *Silver Link* as one of those prime moments in 20th century British railway history when the observer's first instinct was to blink with incredulity. For here, in the darkest days of the war, we had what was ostensibly a mixed traffic locomotive shrouded in a box-like, matt malachite green casing. This rose to a 'widow's peak' above the smokebox, which bore an ownership plate in the shape of an inverted horseshoe, no less.

The numbering system was hard to fathom, conventional spokes on the wheels had given way to circular and pear-shaped holes and pockets which did not carry any balance weights, and

there was even a disc provided to cover the chimney when the locomotive was not in steam. When rumours started to circulate that the locomotive's 'air-smoothed' casing was designed not only to merge with the carriages it was to pull, but also to enable it to go through washing plants with them, sceptics might have been forgiven for wondering whether this machine and its creator were to be taken seriously. Such doubts would probably not have been dispelled by brief enquiry into the designer's background or knowledge of the current state of the Southern Railway. Oliver Bulleid had joined the Southern as Chief Mechanical Engineer at the age of 55 in 1937, his previous post having been as principal assistant to Nigel Gresley on the LNER. Surprise

that he had taken so long to reach the top should, perhaps, be tempered by the knowledge that Stanier was several months older when appointed CME by the LMS. Under Gresley, Bulleid had become heavily involved with development of the 'P2' 2-8-2 and the 'A4' Pacifics. Always an advocate of lively schedules, hard driving and locomotives with plenty of power in reserve, he was an appropriate choice for this work. Eclecticism and a talent for innovation were also strong features in Bulleid's development on the LNER. He was an enthusiastic advocate of large-scale application of welding and, as early as 1929, commented on the desirability of fully-enclosed valve gear (*Master Builders of Steam* H. A. V. Bulleid [Ian Allan Ltd, 1963]).

His already evident Francophile tendencies were consolidated when Gresley sent him with 'P2' *Cock o' the North* to the test plant at Vitry-sur-Seine in 1934. Bulleid was conversant with the work of André Chapelon and this knowledge had already influenced the original design of *Cock o' the North*. He returned from Vitry more convinced than ever of the importance to locomotive design of large steam passages and an efficient exhaust system, ideas which were, of course, incorporated in the brilliantly successful 'A4' Pacifics.

So what was such a man doing on the Southern? Perhaps more importantly, what would it make of him? On taking up office, Bulleid rapidly found that his new employers had, for some years, viewed electrification as their priority. Steam traction had been comparatively neglected, though it was still being asked to fulfil an important function.

Above left:
Channel Packet in original condition at Eastleigh in March 1941. It carried matt malachite green livery with three yellow lines. Sanding was restricted to the front of the middle driving wheels. Note also the original design of big end securing cap. *NRM*

Above:
Following concern at the weight of the first two 'Merchants', the next eight locomotives were turned out with, among other features, lighter, ribbed boiler casing. This feature is visible as blue-liveried No 35004 coasts into Andover with the 12.59 express from there to Waterloo in September 1952. *B. Coates*

Left:
Postwar renaissance. The pioneer 'Merchant Navy', No 21C1 **Channel Packet**, makes a majestic exit from Victoria on 13 April 1946 with a trial run of the 'Golden Arrow' to Dover Marine and back. The locomotive, freshly repainted in malachite green, carries Union Jack and tricolore above the front number and other appropriate embellishments, which are also in evidence on the Pullman cars. *IAL*

Loads were increasing and many of the non-electrified routes comprised stiff gradients. Furthermore, the sheer frequency of the electric services was demanding that steam locomotives show a good turn of acceleration and speed. Nevertheless, the Southern had soldiered on, imposing ever growing demands for passenger work on its stock of 'King Arthur', 'Lord Nelson' and 'Schools' class locomotives. They responded remarkably well to the challenge, though this did not prevent

Maunsell, Bulleid's predecessor, mooting new 4-6-2 and 2-6-2 designs in 1933 and 1934 respectively. Neither of these was acceptable to the Civil Engineer. One also suspects that Sir Herbert Walker, General Manager of the Southern at that time and a great proponent of electrification, would have looked askance at such expenditure.

Hopes of eventually electrifying the whole of the Southern Railway were to remain unfulfilled. Gradual expansion of the electrified network did admittedly take place throughout the 1930s, but it was obvious that a stopgap was going to be necessary for many years

and this would have to be steam. The mere fact that he had come from the LNER, a company which, by 1937, was basking in the reflected glory of the 'A4s' perhaps smoothed Bulleid's path into office. Yet it was also clear that he would need financial support, and the discarding of entrenched attitudes, if he

Below:
No 35008 *Orient Line***, carrying British Railways blue livery with black skirting and fitted with a standard modified three-window cab, heads an Exeter-bound express at Woking on Saturday 18 February 1950.** *P. C. Short*

was to modernise the Southern's steam fleet and put into practice experience gained on the LNER and elsewhere.

The retirement of Sir Herbert Walker, allied to the encouragement gained from the Chairman of the Southern, Robert Holland-Martin, gave Bulleid greater freedom of movement. He had already turned his attention to modifying some of the Maunsell designs. The 'Lord Nelsons' in particular were greatly improved by the fitting of a Lemaître multiple-jet exhaust and new cylinders with improved steam passages. Soon, thoughts turned towards new locomotives, though the Pacific —

No 21C1 *Channel Packet* — which ultimately saw the light of day in 1941 underwent a complex genesis, having also, at various times, been envisaged as a 2-8-2 or 4-8-2.

Beneath its unconventional casing, there was a great deal to interest students of locomotive design and much evidence of Bulleid's receptiveness to new, especially French and American, ideas. The boiler, with its welded steel firebox and thermic syphons, was to prove one of the most formidable steam producers ever seen in this country, even when later reduced from 280lb/sq in to 250lb/sq in working pressure. Allied to this were large bore steampipes and a five-nozzle Lemaître blastpipe. Thought was also given to the fireman's task by the provision of steam-operated firedoors worked by a pedal on the cab floor. The wheels were another departure from convention, being lighter than traditional spoked wheels, giving uniform support to the tyre, and having the tyre shrunk on to a lip, a system later adopted as standard by BR. However, continuity was maintained by the fitting of an LSWR-type steam reverser as used on the 'D15', 'M7' and 'T9' classes. The locomotive also gave a particularly smooth ride, thanks in no small part to the design of the trailing truck, which was later copied almost in its entirety for the BR Standard classes.

Interesting though these features were, it was undoubtedly Bulleid's chosen arrangement for the valve gear on this 3-cylinder Pacific which attracted greatest attention. Clearly influenced by contemporary motor car technology and a desire to do away with the dreadful chore of 'oiling round', he settled on enclosing the valve gear and middle big end in an oil bath between the frames, with two pumps supplying oil at 20psi. The three

Above:
Berkley stoker-fitted No 35005 *Canadian Pacific* roars through Brookwood with the down 'Atlantic Coast Express' shortly after nationalisation. The smokebox roundel is still carried, conflicting slightly with the wording 'British Railways' in Southern Railway-style 'sunshine' lettering on the tender. *R. F. Dearden/IAL*

Right:
A striking picture of No 21C129 at Stewarts Lane in 1947, showing circular ownership plate, route indication lights, disc brackets and original small door under the smokebox giving access to the area immediately in front of the middle cylinder. This was later enlarged considerably. *Ransome-Wallis Collection/NRM*

sets of valve gear were actuated by a crankshaft driven by two chains, one from the crank axle to an intermediate sprocket and the other from the sprocket to the crankshaft. Reciprocating balance was dispensed with, thus obviating hammer blow and damage to track and bridges.

In conjunction with the very straight steam passages to the cylinders, the valve events achieved with this arrangement and the high expansion ratio they permitted resulted in a very free running machine. Certainly, Southern crews now had the potential for far higher speeds than previously. Moreover, they also had tremendous reserves of power to help them over hills and out of the way of other traffic.

Bulleid's light Pacifics, which started to emerge from Brighton Works four years later, shared all the major 'Merchant Navy' features. Indeed, they represented a very interesting concept: that of a locomotive with a 2,000hp capability whose light axle-loading permitted it to run on branch lines as well as work expresses at over 90mph. Whether such a high specification was suited to the duties the locomotives were initially intended to perform — passenger work on the 'withered arm' of the Southern in the West of England — is debatable. They nevertheless soon proved their worth on the Eastern Section, producing performances which were little, if at all, inferior to those of their larger sisters. This was illustrated most graphically in the 1948 Locomotive Exchanges, when Nos 34004 and 34006 excelled in the mixed traffic category, though at the expense of heavy coal and water consumption.

There can be little doubt that, in his Pacifics, Bulleid created locomotives which steamed magnificently, ran fast and hard, were capable of power outputs which occasionally belied their size and endeared themselves to the vast majority of men who drove and fired them. Equally incontrovertible is the fact that the locomotives as originally built were not without their problems. The 'air-smoothed' casing was not conducive to lifting the exhaust under lighter steaming conditions and smoke-deflecting experiments continued almost to the end of the locomotives' working lives. The oil bath was prone to cracking through inevitable flexing of the locomotive's mainframes which formed its walls. The Pacifics had a healthy appetite for coal, though Bulleid himself never seems to have considered this a problem, viewing it as a fair price to pay for the amount of work done. The steam-operated reverser was not universally popular. Although the lack of physical effort required to operate it was appreciated, modifications had to be made to make it more precise in operation and less prone to creep. This feature of the Pacifics was also criticised when No 35022 was tested at Rugby in 1952, though it was felt that the actual degree of creep in the reverser was probably insufficient to have a serious effect on the locomotive's performance in traffic. Overall, the Rugby tests concluded that the 'Merchant Navy' Pacifics were most competent machines, but unfortunately uneconomical in fuel and oil consumption. Inherent weaknesses in the valve gear were also suspected, with the actual cut off not bearing any consistent relationship to the reverser setting,

Top:
Ancient and modern. Unnamed No 21C140 tops Blacksole bank in 1946 with a down excursion train formed of venerable stock. *Ransome-Wallis Collection/NRM*

Above:
The shock of the new as No 21C164 *Fighter Command* contrasts with the more conventional Southern lines of No 902 *Wellington* at Cannon Street on 18 May 1948. *Rev A. C. Cawston/IAL*

though no proper attempt was made to investigate the reasons for this.

By 1952, operating experience and modification had significantly improved the reliability of the Bulleid Pacifics, which were running ever greater mileages between overhaul and matching the best express locomotives of other Regions. Maintenance and fuel costs nevertheless remained high and it was decided that, in late 1955, work should start on the rebuilding of the 'Merchant Navy' Pacifics along more orthodox, BR Standard lines. When No 35018 left the Erecting Shop at Eastleigh on 9 February 1956, it immediately impressed as an extremely handsome locomotive. Gone was the 'air-smoothed' casing, to be replaced by conventional boiler cladding and large

smoke deflectors. But the really significant changes were mechanical. The oilbath and chain-driven valve gear were discarded and replaced by three independent sets of valve gear. Large balance weights appeared on the driving wheels and a new inside cylinder was fitted. The steam reverser gave way to a screw reverser and there was a new design of ashpan which included dampers, a feature never considered necessary by Bulleid. A large number of smaller modifications was also made.

The 'Merchant Navy' class engines as modified were considered by many to be the finest express locomotives ever to run in Britain, giving improved reliability and lower maintenance costs over the original design whilst retaining a great appetite for hard work and fast running. Interestingly, this was accompanied by a continuing ability to burn large amounts of coal, as the tests conducted with No 35020 in April 1956 showed. Many drivers also felt that, whilst being more predictable in their performance, the modified 'Merchants' had lost some of the freedom of movement of the original engines.

The generally positive response to the rebuilding of the 'Merchant Navy' class led to permission being granted in

Right:
At a late stage in the smoke-deflecting experiments, No 34049 is seen at Waterloo carrying a modified cowling. Apparently, little was gained and the modification was not made to any other Pacifics. *Ransome-Wallis Collection/NRM*

Far right:
Before naming, No 34074 takes Shorncliffe by storm on 25 June 1949 with the up 'Night Ferry'. *Rev A. C. Cawston Collection/ NRM*

Below:
A picture which emphasises the revolutionary appearance of the Bulleid Pacifics. No 34002 *Salisbury* breathes light and fire in its namesake city one night in October 1963. The modified big end cap and crosshead are clearly visible. *G. F. Heiron*

Left:
No 35022 *Holland America Line* on test at Rugby in 1952. *J. G. Click Collection/NRM*

Inset:
On trial with the Western Region dynamometer car and an unmodified 6,000 gallon tender, No 35020 *Bibby Line* pauses in Salisbury East carriage sidings on 21 June 1956. *C. F. Verrall*

November 1956 for similar treatment of a batch of the light Pacifics, a total of 60 locomotives eventually being modified in the years up to 1961.

Again, rebuilding reduced repair costs and oil consumption and the engines now burned marginally less coal. Against this must be set reduced route availability because of the increased axle-loading and that other bugbear shared with their modified larger sisters, increased preparation time. Once more, drivers did not feel the modified engines ran as freely, especially on down grades.

Arguments about the respective merits and flaws of the original and

Below left:
The effectiveness of the Giesl Ejector in lifting the exhaust clear of the train is illustrated as No 34064 tears through Farnborough with a 13-coach load in July 1963. *B. A. Haresnape*

Below:
The imposing proportions of the modified 'Merchants' are captured well in this view of No 35001 taking water at Basingstoke on 29 May 1961 whilst working the 15.00 Waterloo-Exeter, with through carriages for Plymouth, Ilfracombe and Torrington. *R. S. Greenwood*

modified Bulleid Pacifics will probably persist for as long as people are interested in steam locomotives. What the original engines had in dash and charisma was matched by the reliability and handsome proportions of the modified locomotives. What is not in doubt is the Pacifics' enduring ability to stimulate debate. Shortly before he died, one of Bulleid's assistants, John G. Click, spoke of plans which were hatched at Eastleigh in the early 1950s for a Mk 2 'West Country'. This would have had fully-enclosed Caprotti valve gear in an oil-bath no longer attached to the frames, so as to avoid cracking. Roller bearings would have been fitted throughout, preparation time would have been minimal and, in an attempt to keep the diesels at bay, locomotives would have been expected to cover at least 300,000 miles between general repairs. As if this were not enough, a distinguished former driver recently defined his ideal Bulleid as having the contours of a rebuild, the valve gear and sump (with modern oil seals) of the original, a screw reverser, a boiler pressure of 265lb/sq in and a Giesl Ejector. (Bert Hooker, *Steam World*, April 1991.) That, he felt, would have given him a world beater.

But enough of conjecture. Perhaps history had the best word, with both modified and unmodified Bulleid Pacifics seeing out Southern steam with distinction in 1967. And, of course, the story does not end there, since Nos 34027, 34092 and 35028 continue to provide us with new feats of haulage over BR lines. Long may they demonstrate what 'Bulleid Pacifics in Action' really means!

Below:
No 35024 *East Asiatic Company* attracts the attention of a youthful photographer at Upwey Wishing Well on a wet July day as it heads an up relief train banked by an ex-GWR 0-6-0PT. The Pacific is paired with a coal- or self-weighing tender.
The late D. Cross

Inset:
Its glory days on the 'Golden Arrow' now behind it, No 35015 *Rotterdam Lloyd* heads a down West of England train — the third vehicle is a Gresley-designed brake — through Woking on 30 July 1961. Platform hoardings advertise shoppers' tickets to London at only 4/9 return (about 24 pence)! *R. S. Greenwood*

Above:
Farnborough witnesses the simultaneous passage of No 34025 *Whimple* with the 06.22 Bournemouth-Waterloo and No 35030 *Elder Dempster Lines* on the 08.33 Waterloo-Weymouth. *J. L. McIvor*

Right:
No 34104 *Bere Alston*, the last Pacific to be modified, is lowered on to its wheels at Eastleigh in 1961. *NRM*

Below:
No 34042 *Dorchester* at speed.
D. Anderson

Left:
No 34098 ascends Hatton bank with a special from Southampton for the FA Cup semi-final at Villa Park on 27 April 1963. Unmodified No 34092 accelerated a 450-ton train to 61mph up this same stretch on 18 June 1988, developing 1,950edhp in the process. *T. E. Williams Collection/NRM*

Centre left:
The exhaust beats down as No 34059 *Sir Archibald Sinclair* storms towards Weston box, in a freezing north wind, with a relief to the 09.26 Weymouth-Waterloo on 28 December 1966. *V. L. Murphy*

Bottom:
Variations on the 'Battle of Britain' theme meet at Basingstoke on 12 September 1964, with Nos 34084 *253 Squadron* and 34056 *Croydon* respectively heading north- and south-bound inter-Regional trains. *R. H. Tunstall*

Right:
Exmouth, one of the most long-lived unmodified 'West Country' Pacifics, traverses the New Forest near Brockenhurst at speed on 10 September 1966 with a Weymouth-Waterloo express. When withdrawn the following spring, No 34015 had covered well over 900,000 miles. Note the battered boiler casing and missing inspection panels. *K. Hale*

Inset:
The Pacifics were even 'modified' — after a fashion! — on brewers' lineside hoardings. *A. G. S. Davies*

Below right:
The down 'Bournemouth Belle' prepares to leave Southampton behind No 34046 *Braunton* on 5 October 1965 as Type 3 No D6509 passes with an oil train from Fawley. *The late D. Cross*

Chapter Two

LIFE WITH THE BULLEID PACIFICS

Dick Hardy

Bulleid had retired before I went to the Southern in 1952, but I had already had a bit to do with his 'West Country' Pacifics on the Eastern Region and had found them exciting machines, which were the unique creation of a unique man. No 34059 came to Stratford in the spring of 1949, for a four week trial, during which time it was driven by the excellent Bill Burritt of Stratford. They worked service trains most of the time, usually accompanied by Chief Inspector Len Theobald, who greatly enjoyed himself. I was at Eastern Region Headquarters at the time and Len and I were very good friends, so it was not long before I met my first Bulleid Pacific and how I enjoyed it!

It must be understood that the GE drivers were full regulator men by train-ing and inclination and that Theobald would not tolerate any other method of operation without good reason. So No 34059 was worked very successfully wide open and on a short cut off, once Bill Burritt had got used to the steam reverser. The results were excellent, as the engine was still maintained by Southern men. The coal consumption was not excessive and so the stage was set for two final trials before the engine went back across the Thames. Trials perhaps, but there was an element of light-heartedness in the proceedings, because L. P. Parker, our Motive Power Superintendent, had made it quite clear that he would not tolerate the perma-nent transfer of Bulleid Pacifics to his Region. As always, he was right, as events were to show.

The Parkeston trial was an educa-tion. Brentwood bank was taken and surmounted before you could say 'Knife', with a fire above the level of the firehole, a phenomenon impossible and undesirable with the LNER design of firedoor. The regulator was wide open with about 25% cut off and Len Theobald saying: 'What's the use of hav-ing 280lbs in the boiler if you don't use

Below:
In 1949, the transfer of 15 light Pacifics to the Great Eastern section of the Eastern Region was mooted. In May of that year, No 34059 *Sir Archibald Sinclair* works an empty stock trial to Norwich out of Liverpool Street past 'B17' 4-6-0 No 61621 *Hatfield House.*
Ransome-Wallis Collection/NRM

Left:
A thrilling view from the footplate of *Sir Archibald Sinclair* in late Southern days, with 'Merchant Navy' *Aberdeen Commonwealth* closing at speed.
S. C. Townroe

it!' The firedoor was kept open all the time, which was also the Southern practice with hard coal, to keep down smoke and avoid blowing off. Once we were over the top, the engine ran very freely on 10-15% except up to Wrabness, where more was necessary.

Coming home, it was my turn to do the work and, had I but known, it was a pipe opener against the day that I was transferred to Stewarts Lane. I remember closing the firedoor leaving Parkeston Quay to get the fire hot and paralysing the place with smoke (which was photographed and published to my detriment). Not using the steam-operated firedoors, I had a perfect trip which terminated as planned at Stratford with an empty tender. In fact, to get to the shed, we had to empty the fireiron troughs of coal on both sides of the tender. In later years, I was to have these cleaned out by the Battersea cleaner boys, but I thought at the time that whoever was responsible for the design of these troughs had never seen a coaling plant.

Next day, with a tender full of splendid hard coal, we took the old 'Spam' to Norwich. We did brilliantly on the way down and the General Manager's saloon was attached for the return journey, his party including our chief. The load was 12 buckeyes and the saloon, and LPP and Theobald had agreed that we were to show our paces. And so we did for the first few miles until, near Swainsthorpe, there was a tremendous roar from the exhaust, followed by

silence and the application of brakes. I was sent back to LPP to tell him that we could neither notch up nor reverse the engine as the steam supply pipe to the reverser had fractured, and that we were going to Stratford in full forward gear. LPP's reply, slightly mellowed by a good lunch and a glass of port, was: 'Hardy, I am sure that Theobald will be able to run to time with that extraordinary machine, even if it will neither start nor reverse'. The incident strengthened his case to wait for larger engines, which duly arrived in the shape of No 70000 and her sisters, for which everybody was profoundly grateful. However, No 34059 worked up to London in full gear and kept time without breaking any records or the fireman's back. I am quite sure that no other locomotive in my experience could have done that, but the Bulleid Pacifics had that unique quality which enabled them, at times, to do what seemed to be impossible.

LPP was proved right even more clearly when the 'Britannias' were grounded in 1952. The 'West Countrys' that came across were all based on Stratford, whilst good 'B1s' looked after the Norwich end. Certainly, the Southern engines could never have been maintained properly by the Stratford staff, with their many difficulties, shortages and strained labour relations. Many are the stories recounted by the Stratford and Parkeston enginemen of empty tenders, of working the 'Hook Continental' to time with a steam

reverser that would constantly slip into full gear, of steam pipe joints and elements blowing, of cracked sumps and, just now and again, the likes of Driver Percy Howard, who maintained that he had never handled a finer engine in his life. But, on a regular basis, no thank you very much, they were far better where they came from! Being at Ipswich at the time, I was only involved when one had to come off its train, as in the case of No 34039. We had to make a swap with the pilot, but the thought of carriage shunting with it was too much for the Ipswich driver. However, there was just enough coal for Bury and back with four coaches and then we were landed with the thing whilst Stratford set our good 'B17' to work on the Southends, effectively sidetracking the Bulleid to their advantage for a few days. But, a few weeks later, I went to the Southern and, at last, began to learn the truth about these amazing machines, for I was responsible for three 'MNs' and 16 'WCs' and 'BBs' and for the men who maintained them and who took them out on the road. I would not have missed it for all the world.

What amazes me about Bulleid is that he was content to remain an Assistant for the best part of 25 years. He never became Mechanical Engineer Doncaster or Stratford or Darlington and so one could be forgiven for thinking that he was born a number two or, perhaps, that the railway he had served so long had failed to develop the career of one who had the hallmark of genius. But, luckily, the Southern Railway Board seemed to want a man who could change things in a difficult world and maybe they got more than they bargained for. Bulleid arrived shortly after Sir Herbert Walker, the legendary General Manager, had retired. The latter was committed to electrification and it is doubtful if Bulleid would have got away with the extraordinary feats of persuasion, of which he was capable, if Walker had remained in office. On the other hand, it is so easy to criticise the bold, the brilliant and the courageous, and here I feel that there was a similarity between Bulleid's approach and that of the great Dr Beeching who, as a young physicist, was promoted to the post of Deputy Chief Engineer of the Armament Design Establishment, which consisted largely of experienced and hard boiled engineers. Beeching refused absolutely to accept a Service demand for any weapon design that sprang from tradition. His physicist's mind fearlessly questioned and probed the fundamentals and paid little attention to custom and tradition. At first his appointment was ridiculed, but the ridicule changed first to sheer awe, then to fascination and finally to great enthusiasm for the approach to engineering of a great intellect. Surely, it was just so with Oliver Bulleid.

With my limited experience of the Board Room, I am unable to say how he persuaded his Directors to agree to the construction of 140 unorthodox Pacific locomotives at a time when there was an acute shortage of material. That he convinced them that Pacifics were a necessary replacement for some of the 'N' and 'T9' class engines that looked after Devon and Cornwall is beyond belief, but the fact remains that

he did. I think that, without a shadow of doubt, Bulleid was a genius. He inherited a well run Department which, through no fault of its own, was falling on idle times and then, having made some changes, persuaded his new people to put into practice his original ideas. He, more than any Chief Engineer in recent times, influenced design on a personal basis at drawing office level. How otherwise could such locomotives have been built, which were so obviously an extension of the personality of their creator? Indeed, one felt that one knew Bulleid through the character of his engines. He too refused to accept traditional practices and some of his ideas were pursued against

advice and without consultation, for he was not particularly interested in the reaction of those poor souls who had to maintain his machines. But we had no real need to complain about that.

So what was the impact of his Pacifics? I can take up the story at first hand from 1952, when the Southern Region had settled down to both nationalisation and to Bulleid's locomotives, without which the Motive Power Department would have been in a parlous state. Do not think, for example, that all 'King Arthurs' were as good as the preserved 'Prile of 7s'. Some of them had got pretty rough and, as the headers and front ends got made up, very sluggish. We had only one

'Schools', the class being on the Ramsgate and Hastings roads. The 'Nelsons' had long since left the Eastern Section and so the Bulleids were essential to the scheme of things.

My first impression of Stewarts Lane was of the clouds of smoke that poured from the big chimneys of the Bulleid engines as their fires were made up for the stern business of getting out of Victoria with a heavy train. I was soon told that the small Pacifics were not fitted with dampers and that 'Mr Bulleid refuses to incorporate a device that prevents an engine generating steam', which, if true, was an extraordinary deduction. Certainly, I was trained never to shut the damper until the end

of a journey, but to work the fire accordingly. This was not difficult when one could make up a fire with hand-picked coal, placed with great care, but far from easy, against the clock, with the short firebox of a 'West Country' and with coal that varied in size and quality. So the engines got it out of their system at the Lane so that they could stand quiet in Victoria.

What was our response to the engines? The 'Merchant Navy', on the road and on its day, could give points and a beating to anything in the country. We paid the compliment to the smaller engines of using them on the heaviest workings, with the proviso that engines with small tenders did not

work the Dover Boats. Which meant that Nos 34065-70 and 34017 were usually on the Kent coast services. As a Shedmaster, I counted myself lucky to have such engines on the strength.

Below left:
Who said steam trains were always filthy? A resplendent No 34048 *Crediton* heads four very smart coaches on an up working near Exeter Central on 14 August 1952.
Rev A. C. Cawston Collection/NRM

Below:
Dignity and impudence at Folkestone Junction in 1948, with No 21C154 *Lord Beaverbrook* on a down train passing 'R1' 0-6-0T No 1340.
Rev A. C. Cawston Collection/NRM

Bottom:
Carrying both front numerals and smokebox number plate, *264 Squadron* roars past Folkestone Warren with an up Continental on 22 June 1949.
Rev A. C. Cawston Collection/NRM

27

They were not invariably reliable, they were not easy to maintain, they were costly, they used a lot of oil, coal and water and, because the drop grates jammed, the fire often had to be thrown out by hand over the top. But our standards were not dictated solely by cost, consumption of coal and water and disposal allowances. The Southern rated the importance of punctuality above everything else and I was accountable for every minute lost by our engines and men. So the ability of these incredible engines to keep time when on the floor for steam, as sometimes happened, was vital to our work. I could never understand how No 34092, not one of our best in 1953, kept time with 450 tons and no more than 160/180lbs steam on the up journey from Dover. I was the struggling fireman, endlessly busy, soaked through, beyond speech. How it was done with three tuppeny-halfpenny little cylinders fed with steam at 120lbs below the working pressure was beyond me! So, good or bad, the Pacifics were our cornerstone.

They varied from No 34090, which was a poor affair, to Nos 34071, 34101, and 34102, which were nearly as good as a 'Merchant'. A great deal depended on the mileage that they had run and how things were going in the smokebox and down below in the sump. No 35028, when still blue in September 1952, was not much good, but came back from Eastleigh a giant refreshed. So did No 35027, but '26 was never quite in the same class. One wonders why this variation was so marked as against other classes, but it was the artisan staff who had to put up with the idiosyncrasies of design and the remarks of the enginemen after they had had a rough trip. For example, superheater elements would blow, and not just one, so that the lot would have to come out and be renewed. The gland where the steam pipes passed through the saddle above the cylinders would give out so that air was drawn into the smokebox, setting up a miniature forge which affected a main

Left:
Platform-end drama at Victoria as *Bere Alston* **leaves with an Ostend boat train.**
J. G. Click Collection/NRM

Top right:
At the start of her journey to the Kent coast, No 34080 74 *Squadron* **erupts out of Victoria in the latter years of steam and apparently causes a wheelchair to be vacated in the process!** *D. Sellman*

Centre right:
A grimy No 34066 *Spitfire* **breasts Blacksole summit with the 'Kentish Belle' in 1956.**
Ransome-Wallis Collection/NRM

Right:
With steam to spare, *Taw Valley* **leaves Whitstable with the up 'Kentish Belle' in 1959.** *Ransome-Wallis Collection/NRM*

steampipe. This would then start to blow and God help the poor stoker!

It is well known that the chain-driven valve gear gave plenty of trouble and that the greatest care was needed to get the right tooth on the main sprocket when reassembling the gear after a No 6 exam. On the other hand, the middle big end was almost always in perfect order and could be put back as it was found. Sumps were prone to

crack, middle piston glands to blow and the middle piston valve operating shaft would get short of oil so that its bushes wore unduly. The Klinger gauge glass joint would blow out and, if this occurred at the shed, rather than cause a delay, a fitter and mate would change the complete unit on the way to Victoria, a nice job on a hot day. And so on and so on. The sumps were topped up each day by the fitting staff, the electric light dynamos were serviced by the carriage lighting people — a typically excellent Battersea arrangement — and the boilers gave us very little trouble. The thermic syphons helped enormously in steam production and the fact that the boiler water was TIA-treated enabled the washout interval to be extended to 56 days. The opinion of many a highly skilled running shed artisan, brought up to work under difficult and cramped circumstances, was that the Bulleid Pacifics, as built, were a

Below:
No thought of Channel Tunnel excavations as No 34101 *Hartland* **skirts the white cliffs at Abbotscliff and heads for Dover in the late 1950s.** *The late D. Cross*

marvellous job whose faults were outweighed by their virtues. But one hopes that Bulleid was grateful to those men in the sheds who were never consulted on novel design features but who had the skill and determination to get things sorted out.

Drivers thought the world of them. They had a job sometimes to see where they were going, but that was only a minor matter to all but the most fussy — not many of them on the Chatham — and, in any case, there were two men on the engine and the firemen called the signals that were difficult for the driver. Firemen were not so sure, especially on a hot day. It was difficult to admire an engine where the fire would disappear going downhill with the regulator shut, but this most certainly happened with the 'West Countrys' and a fireman who let his fire go, down Hildenborough, was in for a tottering time along the 'straight'. But we understood them and they were quite indispensable and I delighted in being responsible for such charismatic engines.

In 1954, I went to Dover and back on No 34091, working a very heavy boat train in both directions. The driver

was Joe Brewer and the stoker Jim Williams, not all that long out of the Forces. I was offered a drive on the down road, which meant that I was going to work coming back. I had invited a certain George Carpenter to travel with us and, at 10.00, we set off for Dover, having a normal run as far as Tonbridge, which was passed on time. So far as I can remember, I was running with about 200lbs in the steam chest and about 25% cut off, quite sufficient to time the train to Ashford without any major alteration in the settings. Jim was maintaining the usual steam pressure with a 'West Country', between 230 and 270. The monitor injector was heavy if every drop of water was picked up. This tended to knock the pressure back, although later I was to learn a rarely practised trick from Bert Hooker which overcame the problem.

We were nipping along quite nicely when George, who has an infinite technical knowledge of the workings of the steam locomotive, said that Mr Bulleid had not designed his machines to be worked like that and we would never see a satisfactory result if I carried on as I was doing. So, after a word with our crew, I opened the throttle wide and dropped the lever over to about 40%. The effect was startling. Jim's enormous fire appeared to take off, although he was able to keep it in place. The engine leapt forward and, after a minute or two, the boiler responded by blowing off from both safety valves at 300lbs with the injector on full bore and the firehole doors wide open. It really was quite an experience but, after a few minutes, we shut up shop and returned to normality, reaching the Marine in peace and quiet.

Joe and his mate had been 'assisted' by a set of Dover men and, on their return, they found that another giant fire had been built up with soft Kent coal. Everything looked just so until we got away up the Chatham but, deep down in that firebed, oh dear me no! In the end, we crept over Shepherdswell with the water in the bottom nut and 100lbs of steam. We rolled to Canterbury and then that fire suddenly came to life and our eventual progress up Sole Street bank was a repetition of the morning's performance. One can only say that the power developed was out of all proportion to the size of the engine, thrilling and unforgettable. I have been involved with the same sort of thing with No 35028 but, with the larger engine, the effort could be maintained for as long as the fireman could

Left:
Blue-liveried 'Merchant Navy' No 35019 *French Line C.G.T.* **makes a stunning sight as it appropriately heads a special train for the President of France, M. Vincent Auriol, near Dover on 7 March 1950.** *Ransome-Wallis Collection/NRM*

● *Dick Hardy began his railway career as a Premium Engineering Apprentice at Doncaster Plant in 1941, learning much of the art of firing and driving steam locomotives from enginemen of great experience. After spending the years 1945-52 working on the GE section, he was appointed Shedmaster at Woodford Halse in 1949, followed by a similar appointment at Ipswich in 1950. In August 1952, fate took him to the Southern Region and he views the 27 months spent in charge of Stewarts Lane shed, Battersea, as in many ways the most rewarding of his career. From January 1955, he was Assistant District Motive Power Superintendent at Stratford, taking charge of the District four years later. After Staff College, he spent 10 wonderful years as a Divisional Manager, his time in Liverpool being particularly memorable. For the last nine years of his time on BR, he was responsible for the recruitment, training and career development of all engineers, junior to senior. Like most Bulleid fans, he is a man of very cosmopolitan tastes, combining a passion for French railways with a love of writing, riding, dressage and cricket. His very active Chairmanship of the Steam Locomotive Operators' Association permits him to continue to meet people from all walks of life and occasionally get to grips with a Bulleid Pacific again on the main line.*

stand it, whereas with the 'West Country' one felt that the world had gone slightly mad and that the fire would eventually get out of control. The rebuilt Bulleids were a sounder proposition altogether but, good though they were, they lacked the panache, the character, the obtuseness, the freedom of movement, the peculiar blows, the all-pervading smell of hot oil and that slightly daring feeling of not being entirely sure what might happen next!

Above:
Royal train empty stock leaving Dover Marine behind the pristine, newly-modified No 34037 *Clovelly* on 28 March 1958. *Ransome-Wallis Collection/NRM*

Below:
***Port Line*, its number chalked crudely on the smokebox door, takes water at Banbury on 12 March 1966 with a football special returning from Wolverhampton to Southampton, which the 'Merchant' worked throughout.** *P. Riley*

501 Squadron takes the down 'Golden Arrow' past Petts Wood junction on 16 May 1959. R. C. Riley

No '85 WORKS THE 'ARROW'

AT REST AND AT SPEED

Below:
No 35005 *Canadian Pacific* draws admiring glances as it awaits departure from Waterloo one day in October 1961.
R. S. Greenwood

Inset:
Speeding through Brookwood in September 1961 is No 34095 *Brentor* with a down Bournemouth train.
R. S. Greenwood

Chapter Three

DRIVING AND FIRING THE BULLEID PACIFICS

Bert Hooker

The boilers fitted to the SR Pacifics were probably the most prolific steam-raisers ever to be placed on locomotive frames in this country. On the 'run of the mill' express engines, the fireman did not have too much scope for varying his firing technique. That is, a fire had to be prepared properly, with hand-picked Welsh coal, and maintained with a view to obtaining maximum boiler pressure when needed. An overloading of the fire or going the other way, allowing the fire to become too thin, resulted in a falling off of pressure and consequently lost time when working heavy trains.

The Bulleids changed all that. Provided the firebars were covered, they would steam. They could be 'nobbed up' (filled with large lumps of coal) or 'blacked out'. If that happened you simply shut the firehole door and asked the driver to 'give her a lift' for a few moments and the needle would rise in the right direction. Compared with a 'Nelson', firing liberties could be taken which would fairly cripple the long firebox engines. In the Indian Summer of steam out of Waterloo, the Bulleids saved the day. Train running would not have reached the level it did in the 1960s if 'Nelsons' and 'King Arthurs'

had still been on the top jobs with the relatively inexperienced firemen of the day. Not their fault, I hasten to add, as they were thrust on to the main line work with very little other work available on which to gain the coveted experience.

In my own case, my first experience of the 'Merchants' was during the war, under blackout conditions, working the 17.00 from Waterloo to Salisbury. The firing technique had to be completely different, switching from the flat blade used on the 4-6-0s to an angled blade in order to direct the coal to the back corners and down the sides. This was most important, particularly with the steel fireboxes. Engine crews were still learning about the new engines and personal experiences were discussed and noted for future use. It did not matter what coal was on the tender. It would be devoured in somewhat larger quantities than usual, but the heavy wartime trains were whisked along, often breaching the 60mph speed ceiling imposed to avoid excessive wear and tear on the track and stock. There was also the ever present need to conserve coal. This was at least thought about by some men conscious of the war effort.

The fireboxes of the 'Merchants' were large, having nearly 49sq ft of grate area and a normal fire of, say, a foot thick under the door and back corners and sloping towards the front of the grate with a depth of about 6in would need at least a ton of coal. But a fire of that description — which I favoured — would produce plenty of hot steam. One would have control of the boiler and the firehole doors could be left open to reduce the smoke nuisance although, at first, officialdom advocated closing them, as the steel fireboxes were of a somewhat unknown quantity. Besides, the excess oil dropping on to the firebox doors after lubricating the operating mechanism would burn, giving off acrid fumes and sounding like a fried fish shop when kept closed, so we kept them open awhile!

When the 'West Country' Pacifics came on to the scene, the firing technique required adjusting again. With their deep fireboxes, which were shorter than on the 'Merchants' — the width was about the same — it was no longer necessary to throw coal across the front of the firegrate. It would feed itself, provided the back corners and under the door were kept well up. But, as no ashpan dampers were fitted, one could soon lose control of the boiler when standing, especially if a full boiler forestalled the usual practice of using the injector to 'keep her quiet' — and no one slept when a Bulleid boiler's safety valves lifted!

Apart from on very hot days, the firing of the big Pacifics was invariably a pleasure to me. I can honestly say that on no single occasion, as a fireman, did I come across a 'Merchant Navy' that gave me any anxiety in the question of raising steam. When I entered the Nine Elms top link in late 1946, going with Driver Charlie Tucker — a true Drummond man — the engine allocated to him and Driver George James was 'MN' No 21C20 *Bibby Line.* I soon began to enjoy the pleasures of running on 'our' engine. On shed days when the boiler was washed out, I would go into the

Left:
Driver Parrinder at the controls of No 34092 in Helm tunnel on 6 February 1982. This was the first occasion on which a light Pacific had traversed the Settle-Carlisle route. *J. Duncan*

cold firebox to clean down the tubeplate with a wire brush, making sure no ash was lodged in the superheater flues or smoke tubes and that the combustion chamber, firebars and brick arch were in good order. I also checked there was no build up of ash in the ash-

pan and that the smokebox was in good condition, not drawing air anywhere. With these basics attended to, great were the benefits on the road. One was sometimes torn between keeping the firebars adequately covered and having the engine blow off, or allowing the fire to develop holes, with consequent detriment to the steel firebox through drawing in cold air.

Just after I started driving, one of the jobs I had was to relieve on the 'Bournemouth Belle' at Waterloo, take the locomotive to Nine Elms and dispose. The train arrived late, with engine No 35011 *General Steam Navigation*,

and Driver George Lark. When I climbed aboard with my mate of the day, George exclaimed to me: 'Just the man! I've had no steam, so look around and find out why'. A marvellously imperious instruction! It seemed strange to me that a 'MN' should be short of steam, especially on the 'Belle', as that was the turn normally booked following boiler washout. However, eventually we arrived in the shed after the disposal work had been completed. I then checked the smokebox for steam blows before my fireman had shovelled out the char. All was in order there, so I instructed my mate to remain on the footplate whilst I ventured into the firebox. The fire had been thrown out, of course, so armed with a 'patent smokebox shovel' — a shunter's pole fitted into an old firing shovel — and a flare lamp, I lowered myself, feet first, into the warm firebox. There was still 80lb/sq in on the clock, so I had cracked the blower in order to keep some breathable air circulating around me. The flare lamp was placed on the central brick arch between the thermic syphons. This allowed me to look at the tubeplate when I stood upright. Well, I had never seen anything quite like it!

The superheater flues were 'blinded', but it was the smoke tubes that made me gasp. For it seemed as though the firebox gremlin had cut blackened oranges in half and stuck them neatly over each orifice, which effectively

GREAT SURVIVORS

Below:
Having worked the 'Night Ferry', *Clan Line* rests at Stewarts Lane shed on 15 June 1958, with No 34092 just visible behind. *R. C. Riley*

Inset:
City of Wells brings a motley rake of stock forming an up boat train past Shortlands junction on 2 August 1958. *R. C. Riley*

blocked off the passage of the hot gasses from firebox to smokebox. Small wonder the engine had been short of steam! The patent shovel now came into use, scraping down the easily removed debris from the tubeplate, which was transferred to the footplate for disposal outside. Of necessity, I did not remain long in that heat, just long

Left:
No 35012 *United States Lines* sweeps gracefully round the curve near Pirbright Junction on 10 September 1966 with the down 'Bournemouth Belle'. *J. L. McIvor*

Bottom:
The 'Bournemouth Belle' at Winchester, with No 35016 *Elders Fyffes* in charge. The locomotive's colour scheme is Brunswick green with black and orange lining. It has lost the casing ahead of its cylinders, but retains 'Devon Belle' fastening strips on its smoke deflectors. *R. S. Knight*

Right:
The ubiquitous No 34013 *Okehampton* shows its handsome lines to good effect approaching Winchfield with the 12.59 Bournemouth-Waterloo on 1 October 1966. It is being worked with a very short cut off. *P. Claxton*

Bottom right:
Smoky progress from No 34036 *Westward Ho* about to cross to the Southampton line at Worting Junction with a Waterloo-Bournemouth train in the early 1960s. *D. E. Canning*

Below:
Glistening in the sunshine, No 35023 *Holland-Afrika Line* departs from Exeter Central with the up 'Atlantic Coast Express' on 5 July 1957. *R. C. Riley*

Inset:
The pioneer 'Merchant Navy', No 35001 *Channel Packet* passes Herne Hill with the 13.30 boat train from Victoria on 10 May 1959. *R. C. Riley*

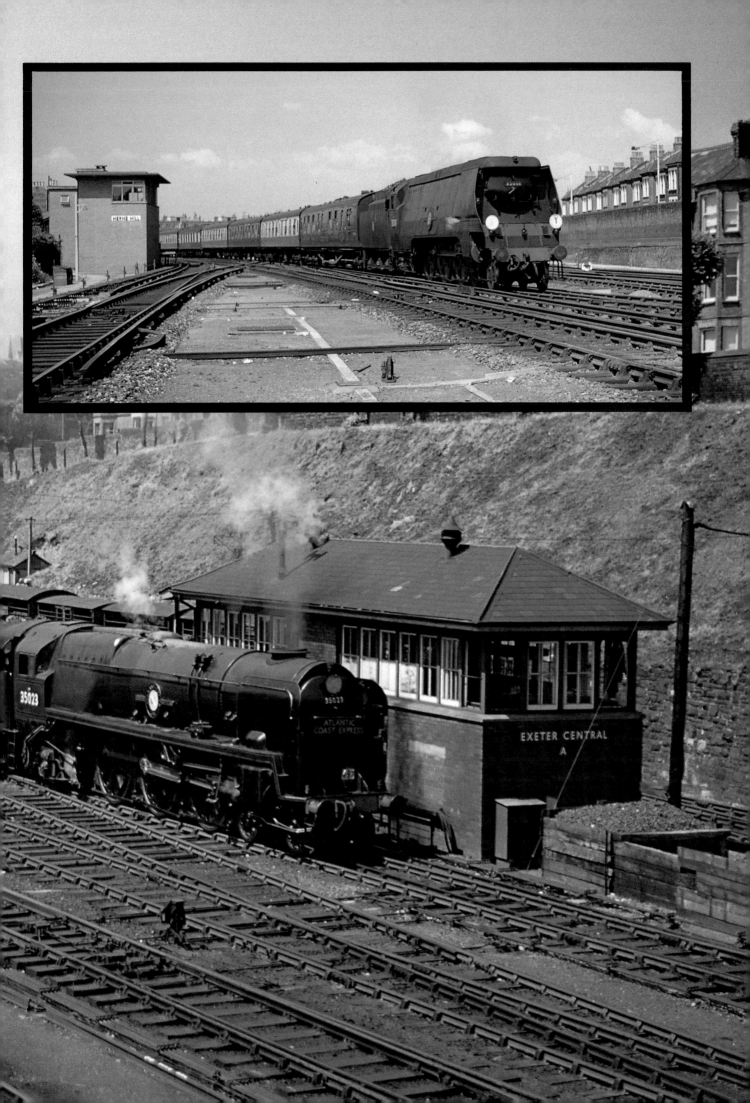

Above:
The rebodied 5,250 gallon tender fitted to No 34031 *Torrington* is clearly visible as the Nine Elms-based Pacific leaves Southampton Central with the 12.35 Waterloo-Weymouth train on 10 July 1960.
R. A. Panting

Right:
No 35013 *Blue Funnel* draws away from Southampton Central and its imposing signal gantry with the 13.30 Waterloo-Weymouth train on 18 March 1967.
J. H. Bird

Above right:
A very smart No 34022 *Exmoor* purrs away from Brockenhurst with the 14.00 Eastleigh-Bournemouth West on May Day 1964. *R. A. Panting*

Top right:
A year and a half after rebuilding, No 35027 *Port Line* approaches Southampton Central with the 11.30 Weymouth-Waterloo in October 1958. *R. C. Riley*

enough to ensure the boiler would steam more freely on the next duty. I kept a couple of the 'half oranges' and gave one to Phil Jarman, the R/F on duty, who eventually passed it on to Alf Oliver — we used to call him 'Socrates' — who used it at his lectures on locomotives. The other I showed to George Lark. His comments were almost to the point of disbelief, but I did remind him that it was up to him to see that his fireman was shown the error of his ways. To my eternal regret, I threw this unusual piece of Bulleid memorabilia away!

The thermic syphons were undoubtedly an asset in the production of steam and served as a most convenient support for the brick arch. One boiler did have the syphons removed for experimental purposes and was fitted to No 35014 *Nederland Line*. The resulting built-up brick arch was nicknamed the 'Dome of Discovery' by one of the main line firemen of the day, one Russell Coffin, now several years into retire-

WEST COUNTRY MEMORIES

Below:
The celebrated No 34004 *Yeovil* at Teignmouth on 2 July 1957 with the 11.35 Exeter-Kingswear, which it worked as far as Newton Abbot. *R. C. Riley*

Right:
Leaving the New Forest, No 34053 *Sir Keith Park* brakes for the Brockenhurst stop with a Waterloo-Bournemouth train on 29 July 1965. *K. R. Pirt*

ment. (The 'Dome of Discovery' was erected for the 1951 Exhibition on the South Bank near Waterloo station.) I did not have any experience of this particular boiler, but was told there was very little appreciable difference in the business of steam raising.

In the field of extracting the best performance from the Bulleids, there were so many things to be taken into account. With a good fireman producing superheated, high pressure steam, I would adjust the cut off to suit the engine, selecting anything from 20% to 35% on the reverser scale, so long as there were no protestations from the front end and general 'feel' of the locomotive. A discerning engineman knows his locomotive and regulates the power required to time the train on the regulator.

On rising gradients, the cut off could be advanced by 2-4% and the regulator opened wider as speed tended to fall. The steam chest pressure gauge was invaluable in this respect. I seldom opened the regulator right out on the Pacifics. It just wasn't necessary under almost every normal condition, but some chaps did so, using a short cut off in conjunction, apparently oblivious to uneven noises up the chimney, along with thumping big ends and driving-wheel axleboxes! Which, in turn, made for a more uncomfortable ride on the footplate, especially noticeable on the Pacifics before rebuilding. Still, the wheels were going round so who cared! I remember Fred Vernon on his 'MN' No 21C18 *British India Line* always using a shortish cut off compared to other drivers in the top link and his engine became noticeably 'rougher' earlier in its career than other engines, bearing in mind that all the Nine Elms 'Merchants' were brand new.

So, I applied the 'know how' learned over the years to the 'Modifieds' and found that the answer was correct. One had to strike the happy medium of driving the engine so that the fireman had the necessary draught on his fire to maintain boiler pressure and yet be economical with coal and water. A contented fireman and a comfortable ride were not to be despised.

Above right:
Light and shade at Bournemouth Central. No 35012 *United States Lines* passes through on an up ECS working on the morning of 4 April 1967, its last month in traffic. *J. H. Bird*

Right:
On a very sunny 10 September 1966, a commendably clean No 34032 *Camelford* leaves Bournemouth Central with a Waterloo express. *R. E. Ruffell*

No 34105 *Swanage* **is extended on Parkstone bank on 15 September 1950 with an up Weymouth express. It is fitted with the earlier design of circular covers — one of which is open — to the sandbox filler chutes.** *H. Weston*

Reduction of the boiler pressure from 280 to 250lb/sq in, in the early 1950s, did reduce boiler maintenance costs, but the incredible feeling of power when one pulled on the regulator handle was subdued. Further reduction came with the rebuilding from 1956 onwards, but at least the reverser now remained where it was set on the 'bacon slicer' and visibility of signals was improved. I estimated that an additional 50 to 60lb/sq in was needed in the steam chests to obtain the same quality of work from the modified Pacifics at, say, a cut off of 20%. There was no doubt about it, the engines were fast, free running, free steaming and comfortable to ride upon. But the rebuilds weren't quite so free running.

Even so, they would quietly run up to the high 80s with 60lb/sq in on the steam chest gauge down Joseph Locke's well-aligned road from Roundwood tunnel to Eastleigh. In contrast, the originals would do this with the regulator almost shut, showing but 20-30lb/sq in on the steam chest gauge. Uncannily effortless running, I wonder what they would have been like on roller bearings?

One had to restrain a Bulleid on running ground rather than 'push' them

Right:
There is considerable activity in evidence on Weymouth shed as No 34061 *73 Squadron* passes with a down holiday special on a September Saturday in the early 1960s. *R. Hewitt*

Below:
No 34094 *Mortehoe* sweeps imperiously through Vauxhall on 20 June 1959 with the 11.15 from Waterloo to the West of England. Note the guard's lookout in the leading brake carriage. *P. H. Groom*

Above:
A down West of England express approaching Battledown flyover on 8 September 1952 behind No 35021 *New Zealand Line*, which is paired with cut-down 6,000 gallon tender No 3342. This tender, the first to be so modified, is still in existence, attached to No 35028 *Clan Line*. B. E. Morrison

Below:
Dusk falls and route indicator lights glow as No 35029 *Ellerman Lines* shunts empty stock at Salisbury near the end of Southern steam. *J. H. Bird*

into speed, and there was nothing quite like them for pulling a train up a bank. When I fired to Jack Swain during the 1948 Interchange Trials on 'MN' No 35017 and 'WCs' Nos 34004 and 34006, that was proved beyond all doubt. Jack said to me at the outset, 'I'm not interested in coal consumption, we'll show them what the engines can do!' I think we did.

The Bulleid Pacifics generated controversy because they were different, but I always felt they were 'good 'uns', as did the vast majority of my col-leagues. There was a reserve of power there to be called upon should the need arise, which wasn't very often in the day-to-day running of the Southern. The rebuilt 'Merchants' were a sheer joy to drive when in good mechanical condition. One unforgettable morning, I had No 35011 up from Bournemouth to Waterloo, hauling 12 coaches, and was called upon to move a failed freight train at Winchester Junction, consisting of 70 empty vanfits and a dead diesel locomotive. The engine moved the whole ensemble without a single slip of the drivers into the goods loop at Wallers Ash, probably with less fuss than an original, and I exulted in the ease with which the job was completed. The gradient was 1 in 250 rising.

During the 1948 Exchanges, the engines were extended more on foreign metals than on our own. Enginemen and observers thought they burnt a lot of coal, to which I reply: 'Extend your engines to match the work of our Pacifics and watch the coal consumption figures rise'. And I have a suspicion the boilers may become 'winded' in the process! I have always maintained a Bulleid boiler is only limited by the rate at which a fireman is able to shovel coal into the firebox. Testing at Rugby did not reach their limit, and the preserved *Clan Line, Taw Valley* and *City of Wells* still demonstrate the qualities of Mr Bulleid's locomotives on the main line. Is it an accident or poetic justice that so many of them are still in existence? As the French drivers would say, 'La belle machine'.

Above:
A dash of colour is brought to Farnborough in September 1952 as blue-liveried No 35007 is followed by five carriages in 'blood and custard' livery at the head of the 14.54 Waterloo-Basingstoke train. *J. M. Davenport*

Right:
An unidentified 'West Country' Pacific heads into a reverse curve south west of Salisbury with a fast freight on 25 September 1954. *G. F. Heiron*

● *Bert Hooker spent 33 years on steam on the Southern, working his way up from cleaner to celebrated top link driver. For most of this time, he was based at Nine Elms depot. He was responsible for many epic runs by Bulleid Pacifics. In 1948, he participated in the Locomotive Exchanges and was fireman on No 34004 Yeovil on the famous occasion when it winded its banker on the climb to Struan on the Highland main line. Very active in retirement, he made history on 13 February 1982 when he became the first man to fire a light Pacific (City of Wells) southbound over Ais Gill summit on the Settle-Carlisle line. He is frequently to be seen on main line excursions hauled by his beloved Pacifics.*

Above:
Paired with a Stanier 4,000 gallon tender and fitted with a Flaman speed recorder, No 35017 *Belgian Marine* hurries the down 'Royal Scot' past Bushey on 13 May 1948 during the Locomotive Exchanges. *D. A. Dant*

Below:
The night of 23 January 1967 finds No 34006 *Bude* — note the extended smoke deflectors — at rest in Salisbury shed. *D. Mackinnon*

Chapter Four

IN BULLEID PACIFIC COUNTRY

Tony Davies BSc CEng MBCS

The following writings relate to a railway scene of individuality, of some thirty years ago, when compared with the everyday, regular-interval scene of the 1990s, diesels and electrics, multiple-units or otherwise. The writer spent all his youthful years, from 1940 to 1970, in southern England and so was heavily influenced by the advent of the Bulleid Pacifics amongst all the wonderful pre-grouping Southern Railway designs, and the enormous variety in the trains themselves. Added to that was a penchant for being on the train itself, preferably in the front carriage, listening and looking, watching out for those mileposts, recording the run and trying to anticipate what might be in the minds of the crew.

In the modern world of unlimited power, where speed is just another parameter in the mechanistics of travel from A to B, it is worth remembering that, in the postwar years, up to 1955 say, speeds of over 80mph, especially when generated by that unpredictable power unit, the steam engine, were exceptional. There was, perhaps, no steam engine quite as unpredictable as the Bulleid Pacific, nor so speedy! Hence their performance, as measured by speed — the only parameter available to the recorder at the carriage window — was a subject of great fascination.

These brief essays aim to describe some performances, both ordinary and out of the ordinary, along their home lines, so full of character, in southern England. Little did I know then how far afield the Bulleids would travel in the 1980s and 1990s.

KENT

Holborn Viaduct, 3am. The confident and strident bark of an ex-SECR 4-4-0 setting off with a train for the Kent coast — the early morning paper train. The historian of the future may well wonder how trains came to depart from Holborn Viaduct at all, let alone a paper train! And what has that got to do with Bulleid Pacifics? When the Pacifics first came to Kent, newly designed and built, for well on 10 years their counter-

Below:
An almost ethereal scene at Earlsfield on 23 January 1965 as the pioneer 'West Country' No 34001 *Exeter* with the 11.30 Waterloo-Bournemouth meets the 09.22 Bournemouth-Waterloo in charge of No 35012 *United States Lines*. The permanent way is very smart. *C. D. Catt*

parts were these veteran 4-4-0s, originally dating from 1900. What a contrast the open cab of one of these veterans with that of a Bulleid Pacific! The Pacifics, barring the few BR Standard engines working in Kent, were the 'last word' in steam power to be seen in that county before the electrification schemes of 1959 and 1961. And as to speed, contrast the rip-roaring dash and fire of a South Eastern 4-4-0 with the air-smoothed quietness of a Bulleid Pacific. No wonder the 'speed merchants' amongst the men that drove the engines of the day sometimes got carried away

The engines of the day. A summer's morning near Rainham, perhaps at Hartlip Hill, a good high vantage point amongst the hop fields. Where the casual observer of today might crave for some variety, on any day in, say, 1954,

the variety in engine power alone was incredible. As for the trains, there were the lordly Kent coast expresses, the local trains, sometimes to Sheerness but more often to Faversham and Dover, the odd excursion train hauled by, perhaps, a 'Q' 0-6-0, and the freight trains, with the occasional Continental GV — oh, yes, and, if you were early enough, the 'Night Ferry'. More easily seen in the morning, when inward-bound to London after the sea crossing to Dover, this was always a magnificent spectacle. The consist of Wagons-Lits sleeping cars, restaurant car and BR carriages was regularly hauled by a Bulleid light Pacific piloted by a 4-4-0; sometimes, when heavily laden, two light Pacifics or, on occasion, even a solo 'Merchant Navy'.

Dover on a summer Saturday in steam days could be a very busy place.

The 'Night Ferry' would go off at about 7.30am, its 4-4-0 and light Pacific struggling into speed on the upgrade past Buckland Junction, at the divergence of the Deal and Canterbury lines. Later on, another light Pacific, this time piloted by perhaps an 'H' 0-4-4T, might be seen taking the Deal road and on up the twisting climb, at 1 in 70, to Guston tunnel. If there was one place in Kent where the light Pacifics sometimes had to be worked exceedingly hard, that was over this ridge between Deal and Dover. Deal could actually be passed at 50mph, but most trains stopped there anyway, and then there was Walmer, with the gradient virtually off the platform end. Most of the expresses from Margate to Charing Cross were heavily loaded through Deal on summer Saturdays; the light Pacifics were limited to nine carriages unassisted. In the up

direction, coming as it did at the start of a relatively long run, it was vital that the footplate was in good shape. No 34025 *Whimple* was on the same up train, nine carriages, on two random Saturdays in 1958 and 1959, and from Walmer, it was simply a case of putting the engine on the 1 in 70 and slogging away at 20-25mph. As always with a modified engine, one sensed there was little room for error.

It is well known that Bulleid set himself the task of producing a machine capable of working 600-ton boat trains from London Victoria to Dover at an average speed of 60mph start-to-stop. That the power was there was unmistakable, that the Bulleids were unable to live up to this yardstick was perhaps a measure of the difficulty of the Kentish lines. True, they became regular performers on the boat trains and

Left:
Against the imposing backcloth of Cannon Street station, No 34025 *Whimple* pulls out with the 17.15 commuter train to Ramsgate on 30 May 1958. Sanding to the leading driving wheels was reinstated on the modified Pacifics and the sandbox can be seen behind the smoke deflector.
R. C. Riley

Above:
A Cannon Street-Ramsgate train at Chatham headed by No 34003 *Plymouth* in 1959.
Ransome-Wallis Collection/NRM

the Kent coast expresses, but the 'Night Ferry' usually loaded to over 600 tons and in general lay beyond their grasp. The regular practice of piloting a light Pacific on this train became a part of the Kentish scene in its own right. Whereas the prewar engines were probably more sure-footed in getting away from the many awkward stops on the Kentish steam roads, when it came to the open road, the sheer power of the Bulleids had no equal for really whipping their trains into speed. The writings of the late Norman Harvey and Cecil J. Allen, eg of *Boscastle* tearing down Sole Street bank with extraordinary abandon, reaching 84mph[1] fully capture the enthusiasm of the time.

One well-known train that was worked by Dover shed, sometimes with a 'Merchant Navy', was the 9.20am Dover Priory to Victoria. This was the crack morning train from Canterbury to London and, with calls only at Chatham and Bromley South, one could usually expect a few lively moments at Faversham as the train tore through at all of 70mph. Stories of 100mph speeds with the Bulleids, on boat trains or otherwise, at Farningham Road are legendary and indeed have appeared in print. The

Below:
With preservation on the Mid-Hants Railway in the distant future, No 34067 *Tangmere* storms the 1 in 67 grade out of Maidstone with a down boat train in August 1959. *B. Coates*

Above:
'West Country' No 34004 *Yeovil* which produced epic performances in the 1948 Locomotive Exchanges, leaves Ashford with a down extra to Deal. Approaching is BR Standard 2-6-2T No 84026 with a train from Margate via Canterbury. *The late D. Cross*

Left:
No 34073 in full cry between Shorncliffe and Sandling with an up express routed via Maidstone East.
Rev A. C. Cawston Collection/NRM

Below left:
501 Squadron arrives at Margate from Victoria on 28 March 1959, with an SECR-designed 'Matchboard' brake coach behind the tender. This combination of coach and light Pacific is still possible on the Worth Valley Railway. *R. C. Riley*

Southern also habitually ran a vast number of additional trains at peak times, when both the Chatham line and the route via Maidstone East were fully utilised. One odd working via Maidstone, that usually ran over a Bank Holiday period, was the 6.26pm Folkestone Central to Charing Cross. I just happened to be at Ashford on the afternoon of 6 August 1957 when the then unmodified No 35028 *Clan Line* appeared with this train. However, with nine carriages (300-310 tons) the running lacked vim and the sharp 20min timing from Maidstone to Otford, pass-to-pass was not kept, with consequent delay inwards to London. But what a glorious noise a Pacific could make when really extended on the fierce climb from Malling up to Wrotham!

The real *magnum opus* of the Kent trains of the time was the 80min 'Folkestone flyers'. These expresses, non-stop to Waterloo, could usually provide plenty of speed thrills. All the necessary ingredients were there one Thursday in August 1956; No 34086 *219 Squadron*, an 11-carriage train (362-390 tons) and just a minute late away from Folkestone Central. The engine was not pressed on the long rise to Westenhanger and actually dropped a minute on the booked time here. Once over the top the crew really let fly, the result being some 12min of sustained running at around 80mph. West of Ashford at that time there was a narrow, single-arched road overbridge. As we approached, at 86mph, Bulleid hooter wailing as usual, and crossed the junction of the Hastings and Canterbury lines, a dining car steward chose that moment to pass through the carriage vestibule — the crash of broken crockery just added to the general din! The two mini summits at Chart and after Pluckley were cleared at the 80 mark and from there to Staplehurst the crew indulged in a perfect hurricane of speed, 85-87mph all the way. The reason for this haste was a 30mph PWS at Marden. On time at Waterloo! While this kind of performance was being enacted day-in day-out, to the casual observer of the time it was steam locomotive running at its best.

So, Bulleids in Kent. Provided all was well, they were complete masters of their work. However, they did have an unfortunate habit of 'sticking' at certain awkward places. One well remembers No 34067 *Tangmere* doing so, westbound at London Bridge, one Sunday in February 1957. On the maintenance side, too, with men used to the simple and robust ex-SECR designs, they may not have been as popular as at, say, Eastleigh. Yet they had their moments of glory and that is how one likes to remember them. In May 1957, 'D1' 4-4-0 No 31545 cut 2min off the 90min schedule of a special to Margate, load six carriages, the last few miles in from Herne Bay being run with all the 'dash and fire' that such an engine could command. How would a light Pacific have performed on a similar schedule, with maybe twice the load?

SURREY AND SUSSEX

3.30am at New Cross Gate. Already one Bulleid Pacific has gone streaming past in the darkness, and here comes yet another. This is any weekday morning in 1962 and these are the Sussex paper trains.

These paper trains were a familiar part of the Southern scene at that time. With usually only a single passenger carriage and a diverse collection of vans, they acquired a reputation for high speeds, particularly in the declining years of steam on the main line. The papers themselves were frequently late in arriving at the main line station and this in itself was a good reason for 'getting a move on', with a clear road and punctuality at the other end of great importance.

On the 'Brighton' section there were two well-known trains from London Bridge, the 3.20am to Brighton and the 3.27 Eastbourne: both Brighton Pacific turns in the late 1950s/early 1960s, though variations on this theme became numerous in the closing years of steam. So, one morning in June 1962, and both paper trains were half an hour late away from London Bridge. With the Brighton train only 5min or so ahead, modified No 34013 *Okehampton* had to proceed decorously out to Earlswood.

Here, vans for Redhill were detached. Now, with the early morning sun just rising and the 'Brighton' well clear, the crew of No 34013 could get cracking. Early morning arrivals off transatlantic flights at Gatwick Airport were treated to the sight of a ghostly but speedy apparition as the Pacific hurtled through, with its short and motley train, at over 80mph. From Three Bridges, and now with only 100 tons behind the tender, the acceleration was phenomenal, but matters were restrained on the descent to Haywards Heath. Once clear of Keymer Junction however, and on the open road, there was another of those tremendous accelerations, to 80 by Plumpton, and 80-85mph well sustained all the way down into the Ouse Valley. Only 15min down by Lewes and a quiet finish on to Eastbourne. Another early morning duty that was frequently worked by a Bulleid Pacific was the 5.08am London Bridge to Brighton via Peckham Rye, Dorking and the Steyning line. No 34013 had also turned up on this train in March 1962. Nothing can quite capture the moments as we thrashed through Queens Road, Peckham, at 45mph, passed Ewell East at 50mph and then thundered down past Ashtead in the early dawn at 60.

The 6.10pm Victoria to Brighton via Uckfield was a commuter train that commanded every respect in the matter of time keeping. The Marsh Atlantics, in the hands of Newhaven men, had coped adequately over the years, but their immediate successors, the ex-LMS 2-6-4Ts, were somewhat lacking in their ability to work so heavy a train to such a fast timing on this road. Then the Bulleid Pacifics came and everybody was happy. No 34013, as well as being a 'goer', had a knack of turning up all over the place, and so it was not surprising to find this engine on this train that same day in June 1962. With 10 carriages (337/365 tons), *Okehampton* was handled carefully in the London area, particularly on the climb from Croydon up into the North Downs. So much so that Oxted, where four carriages were detached, was reached 5min late. Now, on a glorious sunny evening, the pressure was off and the crew started to enjoy themselves. On the long gentle downhill stretch from Hurst Green they were really travelling, and the decompression effect on passing through the twin tunnels at Monks Lane, across the South Eastern line, at 75mph was remarkable. This crew obviously enjoyed fast downhill running, for they went quietly up past Hever and then let fly again, to 66-67 past Ashurst and again on the descent from Crowborough to Buxted.

No 34013 worked the last 6.10 of all, on 10 August 1962, and turned up yet again on a special train which ran this way in February 1966. This latter was in fact the last steam train via Uckfield. Over the years, the light Pacifics became no strangers to the many quiet byroads of Sussex. They occasionally worked the 'Cuckoo' line via Heathfield, where the terrible curving 1 in 50 gradients proved taxing but not insurmountable, and the coastal lines on either side of Brighton. As well as the 'papers' to Eastbourne, they regularly worked holiday extras to/from that point to Brighton, and then on up the main line. The 1 in 88 of Falmer bank, starting as it did from the severe slack through Lewes, was always an interesting problem with a big load. On the 'West Coast' route out of Brighton, on the workings to Cardiff, Plymouth and Bournemouth, they gained a tremendous reputation for fast running amongst the electrics. To experience 70mph through Angmering, eastbound, and then to hear one of these engines fully extended on the last stretch of 1 in 264 from Shoreham up to Hove were moments to savour.

The very ultimate in Bulleid Pacific performance on the 'Brighton' came in the closing months of steam, with 'last runs' from Brighton to Victoria. Both a 'Merchant Navy' and a light Pacific had a chance of doing this, in the up direction, and on schedules of just under an hour with virtually identical loads of eight carriages. Although both occasions were of great excitement, the engines, No 35007 *Aberdeen Commonwealth* in October 1964 and No 34089 *602 Squadron* in December 1966, were working well within capacity and there was really nothing to show between them. An abiding memory of the occasions is how, in Clayton tunnel, with the train now well on the move and at the top of the long 1 in 264 descent towards Burgess Hill, the speed just seemed to go up and up and up. Perhaps, and remembering how those long straight Sussex banks were the scene of some high speed trials involving a 'Merchant Navy' in 1957, the Southern might have had a crack at *Mallard's* record!

Below:
Carrying a long service plaque on its cab side, No 34050 R*oyal Observer Corps* sets out from Victoria with the 18.10 fast to Tunbridge Wells and Brighton one evening in July 1961. *Ransome-Wallis Collection/ NRM*

Left:
Conveying a reception party to welcome the King and Queen of Belgium at the start of their State Visit, No 34089 *602 Squadron* steams past Balham with the 10.20 Victoria-Gatwick Airport special on 14 May 1963. *J. Scrace*

chant Navy' would tackle the hardest bank of all on this road, Seaton, with its long stretches of 1 in 70/80.

Daytime was perhaps a better time for recording those speeds! A rainy day at Axminster in August 1959. The 11.05am train from Waterloo is 30min late. Modified 'Battle of Britain' No 34053 *Sir Keith Park*, 12 carriages (403/420 tons). In those conditions, the engine could not be pressed and so there was a maximum of only 50mph on the short descent to the river bridge. Then, from 45mph past Seaton Junction, the engine was really magnificent, forging her way up the 1 in 80 at a steady 30mph in the pouring rain, with never a sign of losing her feet. Once through Honiton tunnel and over the top the crew really made a run for it. 60mph on the curve through Honiton, 85 in the dip before Sidmouth Junction, 72 round the curves and then flat out for Exeter, sustaining 90mph for two miles or so between Whimple and Broad Clyst. While slightly 'over the limit' for those days, that was perhaps typical of everyday running standards. Axminster to Exeter Central was run in a shade over 31min and, although there are faster runs recorded, it was that slow but steady climb of Seaton bank, in the rain, that was the key to a great performance. In their heyday, of course, the 'Merchant Navies' were expected to start 15 carriage loads (500 tons plus) out of Seaton Junction and then accelerate to that kind of speed[2].

It is right to mention the other side of the coin for once, when the odds were really against the crew. August 1960, and unmodified No 34108 *Wincanton* pulled out of Exeter Central 5min late on the up 'Atlantic Coast Express' with a 13-carriage load, 427/460 tons. A 15mph PWS at Sidmouth Junction meant that Honiton bank had to be climbed at 30mph. So things went on; 2min were dropped on the 101min schedule to Salisbury.

Then, in May 1964, modified No 34040 *Crewkerne* on the 10.30am up, a 10-carriage load, was steaming poorly, but the cheerful Exeter crew (Reg Smallbridge and Bob Oke) strung this rather run-down Pacific along in great style to land up in Salisbury on time. The point here is that, as usual for those times, both of these engines were working through to London, and despite conditions, the Nine Elms men were capable of extracting the usual sustained 80mph running between Basingstoke and Surbiton.

Then there was 1965, the year after steam had finished on the Southern

WESSEX

Again, Templecombe at around 3.30 in the morning might not seem a particularly likely place for watching Bulleid Pacifics passing by, but a restless passenger on the old 1.50am Eastleigh to Yeovil Town could be treated to such a sight every day in the days of steam. This train spent half an hour here, usually reposing in the 'Somerset & Dorset' platform, in order to let the 1.10am Waterloo to the West of England paper train pass by. Invariably then headed by a 'Merchant Navy', the train would tear past on the 1 in 80 up and away over the hill towards Milborne Port — a marvellous sight in the early Dorset dawn. The 1.10am was, of course, an ideal way of starting a long day travelling around the West Country. Sleep was

Above:
By the time No 34044 *Woolacombe* led an up parcels train from Portsmouth through Cosham — 21 February 1967 — there remained only three steam workings daily from Portsmouth. *J. A. M. Vaughan*

always a problem. One would sit there, trying to doze off, while the pace of the train quickened on yet another long descent. Then, after achieving some very high maximum speed, sounds and sensations magnified by the blackness of the night, all the tumult would dwindle away on yet another long soaring climb to yet another unknown summit. And so on, down to Exeter. There were unadvertised stops at Yeovil Junction, to detach vans, and Axminster. By now, one was more or less sufficiently awake to take an interest in how our 'Merlines west of Exeter, and, except in emergency, on the Exeter road itself. However, the holiday requirements of Exmouth and Sidmouth meant that extra trains were still needed for those resorts and, although the schedules were laid down on the basis of diesel haulage, these Saturday trains were regularly steam-worked. So one day saw No 34015 *Exmouth* setting off from Sidmouth Junction 15min late and putting up yet another run in the highest Bulleid Pacific traditions. Nine minutes were gained to Salisbury alone, with speeds in the 80s at the usual points, and No 34089 passing by at Tisbury, on the Brighton to Plymouth through train, to make it seem like the old days.

One day in June 1962, light Pacific No 34055 *Fighter Pilot* was on the Plymouth to Brighton, 13min late away from Salisbury and with an 11-carriage load. Down that long tempting straight from Alderbury Junction to Romsey, the speeds were not exceptional for the time, with 74mph at Dean and 5min gained to Southampton. What followed, with a train weighing just 400 tons tare, was positively frightening. The Netley line abounds in sharp curves followed by steep ascents, not the easiest line for skilful handling of a steam locomotive. Once clear of the curves at Northam Junction, St Denys and Woolton, the crew really got going. On the 1 in 97 up past Sholing, *Fighter Pilot* must have been flat out, to judge from that not too familiar note of desperation in the exhaust beat. Yet she kept her feet here and from 36mph over the top there was a brief spell at 60-63mph after Netley before braking for the sinuous descent to Bursledon. As fast as possible over the river bridge here and then No 34055 was opened up again for the following two miles up to Swanwick. Here, speed was sustained at 37mph, and with 64mph down the other side Fareham was reached in 22min. Another 5min gained. On an earlier run, in 1958, and with a lighter load, the same engine had run this stretch in 26min — just an idea of what the Pacifics could do when really under pressure. After detaching the

Above right:
The 09.33 Waterloo-Bournemouth excursion train, diverted from the main line because of engineering works in the Winchester area, passes Bursledon, having travelled via Guildford, Havant, Cosham and Fareham, with 'WC' No 34008 *Padstow* in charge on 15 April 1967. *J. H. Bird*

Right:
The Bulleids were popular performers on railtours. A creditably smart No 34019 *Bideford* works past Redbridge with a Warwickshire Railway Society special from Birmingham Moor Street to Weymouth on 5 September 1965. It was never regular practice to clean the top of the Pacifics' boiler casing. The inspection panel over the clack valves is missing. *B. Stephenson*

Above:
No 34089 *602 Squadron* slips as it restarts a 12-coach RCTS special from Fareham for the run to Wareham via the Netley line on 18 June 1967. *J. H. Bird*

Left:
Coasting down past Midford goods yard on the Somerset & Dorset on 25 July 1953 is No 34040 *Crewkerne* with the 09.05 Bristol-Bournemouth. The small hut housed the ground frame controlling access to the yard. This locomotive was one of four 'West Country' Pacifics allocated to Bath in 1951. *I. Peters*

Below left:
Stained by hard work and neglect, former Bath-based No 34043 *Combe Martin* recovers from a signal check at Hinksey near Oxford on Saturday 15 August 1959 with the 09.30 Bournemouth West-Birkenhead. *J. D. Edwards*

Portsmouth portion, No 34055 simply cruised on eastwards, holding just under 70mph on the long straight stretches past Bosham, and on time at Chichester!

With light loads, the Pacifics were soon having a crack at the hallowed 15min timing between Dorchester and Wareham, but in the opposite direction[3]! Here again, the gentle slope from Wool up to Moreton was stimulus enough for many a Pacific to be opened out. As well as the familiar main lines,

Above:
**On 29 August 1964, No 34082
615 Squadron heads a Waterloo-Exeter
express at an unspecified location.** *M.
Dunnett*

the Pacifics found themselves — 'Merchant Navy' class excepted — just as much at home on the Portsmouth Direct, when diverted from the main line, on the 'old road' via Ringwood or that quiet backwater of a line from Bournemouth to Salisbury via Fordingbridge. The latter line always seemed to be just a useful means of transferring light Pacifics between Salisbury or Bournemouth sheds, if one or the other happened to be short of those engines. However, there is a very well-known story relating to No 34102 *Lapford,* on which engine the crew found themselves totally out of coal, near Downton, one day in December 1960, while working the diverted 'Pines Express' through from Birmingham New Street. And with Parkstone bank ahead!

Modified No 34047 *Callington* looked very impressive standing at Bournemouth West one day in July 1961, at the head of the 9.25am to Manchester via the Somerset & Dorset, a 12-carriage load of around 400 tons again. There had to be very competent locomotive work in handling a train of this weight over the undulating road that characterised the southern part of the Wessex S&D. Nevertheless, and with a final burst of 65mph at Cole, before easing for the curves over the GW main line, Evercreech Junction was

reached 5min early. Stories of the Bulleid Pacifics on the Wessex S&D, and the difficulties they could get into with slipping, are legion. Even with relatively light loads, pilot assistance was the norm north of Evercreech — yet if the conditions were favourable, one might by chance witness some phenomenal power output. One day in September 1960, modified No 34042 *Dorchester*, with '2P' 4-4-0 No 40700 as pilot, set off from Evercreech Junction on a nine-carriage train. As usual, 'difficulties were encountered' on the first stretch of 1 in 50 up to Shepton Mallet. Having covered the first three miles in about 15min — which may not sound brilliant to the reader, but is a different matter out on the open road — the crews were by now probably pretty fed up. However, on the short downhill stretch of line past Shepton Mallet, both engines were opened right out, to go powering away up the following last stretch of 1 in 50 at a steady 37mph. On the curves after Winsor Hill tunnel, the speed dropped back to the 30 mark and No 34042 started to slip, but the sheer impetus of the assault car-

ried them safely over the top at Masbury. The four miles from Shepton took just 7min. Seven minutes of magic, and on time at Bath.

DEVON AND CORNWALL

If the effect of the Bulleid Pacifics on the men at the Kentish sheds of, say, Ramsgate and Dover, was fairly predictable, the effect at the other end of the system, Wadebridge, must have been positively electrifying! Wadebridge shed handled all the Southern duties at the western end of the North Cornwall line, one of the long 'withered arms' of the old Southern system west of Exeter. This comprised the lines to Ilfracombe and Torrington (still extant as far as Barnstaple), Plymouth, Padstow and Bude. The light Pacifics became a familiar part of the scene on those lines in the postwar years; modified engines were prohibited on the North Cornwall line (and to Plymouth until 1960) and the 'Merchant Navies' altogether west of Exeter (except on the GW route).

On the Ilfracombe line, they had the tremendous task of handling the 'Devon Belle' all-Pullman train, with banking or pilot assistance from Barnstaple over the heavy grades on either side of the Mortehoe summit. On those grades, of 1 in 36 or 1 in 40, it was generally just one long slog from start to stop. Any mention of Pullmans and

Far left:
The burnished front end fittings suggesting
it had probably seen recent royal train
service, No 35023 negotiates Worting
Junction with the up 'ACE' on 27 July 1952.
This had been the last 'Merchant' to carry
malachite green livery.
Rev A. C. Cawston Collection/NRM

Centre left:
Immaculate in standard blue livery with
black and white lining — a scheme about
to be abandoned because it did not wear
well — No 35020 *Bibby Line* passes Worting
Junction on Saturday 21 July 1951 with the
down 'ACE'. *E. D. Bruton*

Left:
On the morning of 11 March 1961,
No 34099 *Lynmouth* gets to grips with an
up fitted freight at Salisbury. *J. C. Haydon*

Below:
Judicious use of the sanders helps
No 34050 *Royal Observer Corps* away from
Salisbury with a Waterloo-bound express in
the early 1950s. *G. F. Heiron*

Right:
The 'Devonshire Rambler' excursion of
26 June 1966 is about to enter Buckhorn
Weston tunnel behind No 35023 *Holland-Afrika Line*. *I. Peters*

Bulleid Pacifics in Devon just cannot go by without reference to the remarkable feat of the No 35023 when working an Ian Allan Pullman special from Plymouth to Paddington in September 1958[4]. Passing Plympton at the distinctly high speed, for those days, of 55mph, Driver Gidley then found himself unable to open the regulator further so as to hold the speed up the two miles at 1 in 42 of Hemerdon bank. The speed in fact dropped to 14mph before, with assistance from his fireman, Gidley was successful, whereupon No 35023 then accelerated to 24mph while still fully on the 1 in 42, and with 318/340 tons behind the tender. No 35023 worked the train successfully onwards to Paddington. This little exploit probably confirmed, in the minds of Exeter enginemen, that the 'Merchant Navy' class stood head and shoulders above the GWR 'King' class as far as performance was concerned[5].

The hardest task for the light Pacifics in the far west was the daily Brighton to Plymouth train, via Exeter, Okehampton and Tavistock. With nine or 10-carriage loads, this demanded continuous effort up the long climbs on either side of the 950ft summit near Meldon Junction, where the Padstow and Bude line diverged from the Plymouth road. On summer Saturdays, there were even one or two trains booked non-stop from Exeter through to Halwill Junction, where the Padstow and Bude lines finally diverged. With a heavy train, this could be a very tough task indeed. No 34075 on a nine carriage train in August 1959 was down to 30mph on the banks and from 63mph at North Tawton passed Okehampton at 36mph.

At the height of the wartime bombing in Plymouth, in 1941, matters were such that, on certain occasions, even the 'Cornish Riviera Express' was diverted via Wadebridge. Here the train had to be split, because of the gradients and the limited power of the engines then available, before the arrival of Bulleid Pacifics. Wadebridge men, moreover, rarely worked east of Launceston and were more used to the stalwart 'N' Moguls and ex-LSWR 4-4-0s, as well as the Beattie well-tank freight working to Wenford Bridge. On the North Cornwall line, the opportunities of utilising the power of the Pacifics in the upper reaches of their speed range were rather limited. Yet the sparks could fly on that long stretch of line reaching out from Okehampton into those Cornish lands still then of great character. Contemporary accounts of the early 1950s reveal that there was one driver on the line who would

attempt speeds of around 80mph on certain sections. This was interesting, since the overall speed limit happened to be 55mph. While the line west of Meldon Junction was single throughout, with passing loops at the stations, experience showed that such high speeds were perfectly possible and safe in the right places.

A Friday evening in August 1963, with the 11.00 ex-Waterloo, No 34072 *257 Squadron*, eight carriages (270/285 tons) and 3min late away from Launceston. Here the load and a slippery rail meant the engine could not be pressed on the ascent to Otterham and, despite some heavy working after Tresmeer, the booked time was only just kept.

Above:
A Sunday morning stopping train from Exeter curves away from Yeovil Junction at 12.37 on 20 October 1963 and heads for Yeovil Town behind No 34070 *Manston*. *M. Pope*

Otterham to Camelford, and on to Delabole, past the gaping hole of the slate quarry, were run quietly. Still 3min late away from Delabole — something had to be done! Words are totally inadequate to describe the sheer ferocity involved in covering the next four miles in 5min start-to-stop. With this big train, No 34072 was simply let rip, the train twisting and turning on those wide curves down those long, sloping, sunlit Cornish fields to reach a hurricane-like maximum of 75mph. It was the same story again from Port Isaac Road, this time the sensations of speed heightened by the narrow rock cuttings on either side of Trelil tunnel. With 64mph before St Kew Highway, 34mph through that station (change the tablet!) and all but 70mph on down the Allen Valley, Wadebridge was reached on time. No wonder the Wadebridge men made the most of this short stretch

Above:
A Sunday morning stopping train from Exeter curves away from Yeovil Junction at 12.37 on 20 October 1963 and heads for Yeovil Town behind No 34070 *Manston*. *M. Pope*

of line. It was the summer Saturday up 'Atlantic Coast Express' that really tested the power of the Bulleid light Pacifics on the North Cornwall road. August 1961, and No 34035 *Shaftesbury* had a 10-carriage load (340/360 tons) to handle up those fearsome 1 in 73 hills towards Camelford. Not surprisingly, despite reaching speeds of 30mph between the stations, the engine was consistently behind the clock in the early stages of the run.

Left:
The fireman judges it a good moment to clean his window as No 34107 *Blandford Forum* clambers out of Buckhorn Weston tunnel with a heavy up freight on 20 March 1962. Like Nos 34014 and 34023, this 'West Country' Pacific carried two-line nameplates. *Rev R. T. Hughes*

Right:
A favourite and much-travelled member of its class, No 34057 *Biggin Hill* scurries along near Yeovil with the 10.25 Yeovil (Pen Mill)-Weymouth on Sunday 6 September 1964. *G. T. Robinson*

11min late away from Launceston, Waterloo some 220 miles distant. Once again, something had to be done! Out to Ashwater the footplate was put into good order. Then, from 26mph, the regulator was opened wide. With cut-off unchanged at 40%, *Shaftesbury* accelerated this big train to 52mph and then, on 1 in 82/73 up, speed gradually fell away to 41mph before easing for the Halwill stop. Three full minutes were gained to Halwill and, with another minute gained at Okehampton, there were then all those downhill miles to Exeter. As an example of what could happen here, one Tuesday in August 1960, No 34038 *Lynton* had acquired a similar load by Oke-

Left:
Bloodied but unbowed, No 34051 *Winston Churchill* departs Axminster for Exeter in August 1957. *H. Sagar*

Below:
The 7 March 1965 saw No 35022 *Holland America Line* at Seaton Junction heading the LCGB 'East Devon Railtour'. On 4 September 1964, this locomotive had hauled the last down 'ACE' to the tight 80min Waterloo-Salisbury schedule. *D. B. Clark*

Below right:
Evoking memories of holiday journeys in Devon, No 35004 *Cunard White Star* passes Seaton Junction with a Waterloo express about 1960. *D. Sellman*

hampton, again after working up from Padstow. Even so, the acceleration down the 1 in 77 was so rapid that the engine could be eased well above the Sampford Courtenay curves. Then, with that long tantalising straight on towards North Tawton coming into view, there was a glorious gallop in the low 80s, the usual bump at North Tawton and rocketing round the Bow curves. A hectic few minutes, all too brief! Five minutes were gained to Yeoford and, after the stop here, another 80 was notched up past Newton St Cyres. Typical everyday work by a Bulleid on this road.

Finally, perhaps the journey of all time, with a Bulleid light Pacific deep into Cornwall, down the Cornish main line from Plymouth to Penzance no less! May 1964. With a seven carriage train, a load well within 'Castle' capacity for that road, Driver Stanbury and Fireman Hainsworth from the GW Plymouth Laira shed covered themselves with glory. No 34002 *Salisbury* tackled those unfamiliar Cornish banks with the same vigour that she and all her companions had displayed, in true Bulleid fashion, all over southern England throughout the previous 20 years. 15min late away from Plymouth on the outward run, on time by Truro, with again and again a deafening exhaust as that lightweight load was sped up those long twisting banks. Then, late away again from Penzance, after the farewell celebrations, *Salisbury* tore away past

Marazion, 45mph here, to finish up at Redruth on time. So it went on, on a golden spring evening, large crowds at all the stations and a real sense of sadness as steam made its final bow on the Cornwall main line west of Truro. How fitting that one of Mr Bulleid's light Pacifics should have had this last word before the end of steam!

REFERENCES

[1]*Railway Magazine*, November 1951.
[2]*Railway Magazine*, March/April 1946.
[3]*Bulleid's Pacifics*, D. W. Winkworth (George Allen & Unwin Ltd, 1974).
[4]*Trains Illustrated*, December 1958 (also *Bulleid's Pacifics*, Table 91).
[5]*Bulleid of the Southern*, H. A. V. Bulleid (Ian Allan Ltd, 1977) p208.

ACKNOWLEDGEMENTS

The opportunity is taken of acknowledging the initiatives of the railtour officers of the following societies:
Locomotive Club of Great Britain
Plymouth Railway Circle
Railway Correspondence and Travel Society
Southern Counties Touring Society
Stephenson Locomotive Society

Right:
Super power for the 08.25 Plymouth-Waterloo near Honiton on 5 September 1964, with Nos 34106 *Lydford* and 34079 *141 Squadron* in harness. *G. T. Robinson*

Centre right:
In a delightful pastoral setting, No 34065 *Hurricane* draws near to Sidmouth Junction with the 13.10 Exeter Central-Yeovil. *J. Parsons*

Far right:
Framed skilfully by the photographer, No 35026 *Lamport & Holt Line* romps out of Exeter Central with the return working of a privately-sponsored tour from Waterloo on 15 October 1966. *R. L. Sewell*

Below:
Shadows lengthen at Exeter Central on Sunday 9 July 1961 as No 35019 *French Line C.G.T.* and an unidentified sister await departure with Waterloo trains.
R. S. Greenwood

Bottom right:
A vintage Rover competes for attention with No 34072 *257 Squadron* descending the 1 in 37 spur from Exeter Central to St David's with the Ilfracombe and Torrington portion of the 11.00 from Waterloo on Sunday 14 June 1959. *M. Mensing*

Bottom left:
Exeter St David's in 1964, with No 34020 *Seaton* about to depart on an Ilfracombe-Exeter Central train. *M. Pope*

Left:
With a more pronounced curve to its smoke deflectors than was normal, No 34072 leaves Exeter St David's with the 07.50 Yeovil-Barnstaple on 13 July 1963. *R. C. Riley*

Above:
'W' 2-6-4T No 31911 rests in the bankers' siding near Exeter St David's before assisting a train up to Exeter Central as No 34024 *Tamar Valley* passes with an up four-coach working on 13 July 1963. *R. C. Riley*

Right:
Long before anyone thought of employing American-built diesels on stone trains in the West Country, No 34021 *Dartmoor* passes Yeoford in the up direction with a ballast working in July 1951. The engine still carries the casing in front of the cylinders. *The late D. Cross*

Centre right:
Ilfracombe near Tavistock on 14 April 1951 with a down train. *Russell-Smith Collection/NRM*

Below:
Under a beautiful sky, No 34017 *Ilfracombe* passes Umberleigh with the westbound 'Devon Belle' on 20 August 1952. The locomotive still carries its original narrow, flat-fronted cab. *Rev A. C. Cawston Collection/NRM*

Appendix One

'MERCHANT NAVY' CLASS

No	Name	Built	Renumbered	Date Renumbered	Rebuilt	Withdrawn	Final Mileages*
21C1	Channel Packet	6/1941	35001	10/1949	8/1959	11/1964	1,095,884
21C2	Union Castle	6/1941	35002	1/1950	5/1958	2/1964	1,101,914
21C3	Royal Mail	9/1941	35003	5/1948	8/1959	7/1967	1,131,793
21C4	Cunard White Star	10/1941	35004	4/1948	7/1958	10/1965	1,131,417
21C5	Canadian Pacific	12/1941	35005	4/1948	5/1959	10/1965	976,806
21C6	Peninsular & Oriental S.N.Co.	12/1941	35006	12/1948	10/1959	8/1964	1,134,319
21C7	Aberdeen Commonwealth	6/1942	35007	12/1948	5/1958	7/1967	1,318,765
21C8	Orient Line	6/1942	35008	7/1949	5/1957	7/1967	1,286,418
21C9	Shaw Savill	6/1942	35009	8/1949	3/1957	9/1964	1,127,452
21C10	Blue Star	7/1942	35010	12/1948	1/1957	9/1966	1,241,929
21C11	General Steam Navigation	12/1944	35011	11/1948	7/1959	2/1966	1,069,128
21C12	United States Lines	1/1945	35012	3/1949	2/1957	4/1967	1,134,836
21C13	Blue Funnel	2/1945	35013	7/1948	5/1956	7/1967	1,114,658
21C14	Nederland Line	2/1945	35014	5/1949	7/1956	3/1967	1,062,394
21C15	Rotterdam Lloyd	3/1945	35015	6/1949	6/1958	2/1964	813,950
21C16	Elders Fyffes	3/1945	35016	10/1948	4/1957	8/1965	900,637
21C17	Belgian Marine	4/1945	35017	4/1948	3/1957	7/1966	1,017,754
21C18	British India Line	5/1945	35018	5/1948	2/1956	8/1964	956,544
21C19	French Line C.G.T.	6/1945	35019	4/1948	5/1959	9/1965	947,344
21C20	Bibby Line	6/1945	35020	5/1948	4/1956	2/1965	981,479
35021	New Zealand Line	9/1948			6/1959	8/1965	859,661
35022	Holland America Line	10/1948			6/1956	5/1966	903,542
35023	Holland-Afrika Line	11/1948			2/1957	7/1967	941,326
35024	East Asiatic Company	11/1948			4/1959	1/1965	839,415
35025	Brocklebank Line	11/1948			12/1956	9/1964	884,081
35026	Lamport & Holt Line	12/1948			1/1957	3/1967	858,784
35027	Port Line	12/1948			5/1957	9/1966	872,290
35028	Clan Line	12/1948			10/1959	7/1967	794,391
35029	Ellerman Lines	2/1949			9/1959	9/1966	748,343
35030	Elder-Dempster Lines	4/1949			4/1958	7/1967	850,876

The entire class was built at Eastleigh Works. *It should be noted that the official recording of mileages for the Bulleid Pacifics ceased late in 1964, after which records were kept by the motive power depots. It is probable that those engines which remained in traffic until 1967 ran a somewhat higher mileage than indicated.

Right:
One of the distinctive 'Merchant Navy' nameplates. Steps were taken to ensure that the flags flew the right way on each side of the locomotive. *NRM*

Appendix Two

'WEST COUNTRY' AND 'BATTLE OF BRITAIN' CLASSES

No	Name	Built	Renumbered	Rebuilt	Withdrawn	Final Mileages*
21C101	Exeter	5/1945	3/1949	11/1957	7/1967	1,079,957
21C102	Salisbury	6/1945	10/1948		4/1967	1,003,613
21C103	Plymouth	6/1945	4/1948	9/1957	9/1964	811,674
21C104	Yeovil	7/1945	5/1948	2/1958	7/1967	920,972
21C105	Barnstaple	7/1945	5/1948	6/1957	10/1966	837,332
21C106	Bude	7/1945	5/1948		3/1967	1,099,338
21C107	Wadebridge	8/1945	3/1949		10/1965	823,193
21C108	Padstow	9/1945	3/1949	6/1960	6/1967	961,734
21C109	Lyme Regis	9/1945	4/1949	1/1961	10/1966	959,762
21C110	Sidmouth	9/1945	1/1950	1/1959	3/1965	922,906
21C111	Tavistock	10/1945	5/1948		11/1963	800,455
21C112	Launceston	10/1945	6/1948	1/1958	12/1966	847,523
21C113	Okehampton	10/1945	6/1948	10/1957	7/1967	944,928
21C114	Budleigh Salterton	11/1945	10/1949	3/1958	3/1965	837,477
21C115	Exmouth	11/1945	4/1948		4/1967	903,245
21C116	Bodmin	11/1945	7/1948	4/1958	6/1964	811,674
21C117	Ilfracombe	12/1945	5/1948	11/1957	10/1966	856,641
21C118	Axminster	12/1945	6/1948	9/1958	7/1967	974,317
21C119	Bideford	12/1945	4/1948		3/1967	701,316
21C120	Seaton	12/1945	4/1948		9/1964	789,688
21C121	Dartmoor	1/1946	7/1948	12/1957	7/1967	950,142
21C122	Exmoor	1/1946	6/1948	12/1957	4/1965	793,647
21C123	Blackmore Vale	2/1946	4/1948		7/1967	921,268
21C124	Tamar Valley	2/1946	6/1948	2/1961	7/1967	839,964
21C125	Whimple	3/1946	9/1948	10/1957	7/1967	872,938
21C126	Yes Tor	3/1946	5/1949	2/1958	9/1966	916,244
21C127	Taw Valley	4/1946	7/1948	9/1957	8/1964	764,316
21C128	Eddystone	4/1946	12/1948	8/1958	5/1964	851,549
21C129	Lundy	5/1946	2/1949	12/1958	9/1964	828,489
21C130	Watersmeet	5/1946	11/1948		9/1964	744,279
21C131	Torrington	6/1946	1/1949	11/1958	2/1965	841,182
21C132	Camelford	6/1946	4/1948	10/1960	10/1966	853,398
21C133	Chard	7/1946	12/1948		12/1965	884,916
21C134	Honiton	7/1946	7/1948	8/1960	7/1967	942,133
21C135	Shaftesbury	7/1946	1/1949		6/1963	764,306
21C136	Westward Ho	7/1946	5/1948	8/1960	7/1967	894,546
21C137	Clovelly	8/1946	3/1949	3/1958	7/1967	810,658
21C138	Lynton	9/1946	2/1949		6/1966	819,984
21C139	Boscastle	9/1946	6/1948	1/1959	5/1965	745,508
21C140	Crewkerne	9/1946	10/1948	10/1960	7/1967	769,624
21C141	Wilton	10/1946	1/1949		1/1966	626,417
21C142	Dorchester	10/1946	5/1948	1/1959	10/1965	726,761
21C143	Combe Martin	10/1946	9/1948		6/1963	749,112
21C144	Woolacombe	10/1946	12/1948	5/1960	5/1967	894,998
21C145	Ottery St Mary	10/1946	1/1949	10/1958	6/1964	761,465
21C146	Braunton	11/1946	1/1949	2/1959	10/1965	779,210
21C147	Callington	11/1946	1/1949	11/1958	6/1967	845,991
21C148	Crediton	11/1946	8/1948	3/1959	3/1966	847,615
21C149	Anti Aircraft Command	12/1946	4/1949		12/1963	723,947
21C150	Royal Observer Corps	12/1946	1/1949	8/1958	8/1965	796,814
21C151	Winston Churchill	12/1946	11/1948		9/1965	807,496
21C152	Lord Dowding	12/1946	2/1949	9/1958	7/1967	936,502
21C153	Sir Keith Park	1/1947	6/1949	11/1958	10/1965	825,317
21C154	Lord Beaverbrook	1/1947	3/1949		9/1964	737,443
21C155	Fighter Pilot	2/1947	7/1949		6/1963	706,607
21C156	Croydon	2/1947	5/1948	12/1960	5/1967	957,081
21C157	Biggin Hill	3/1947	6/1949		5/1967	939,597
21C158	Sir Frederick Pile	3/1947	12/1948	11/1960	10/1964	812,586
21C159	Sir Archibald Sinclair	4/1947	3/1949	3/1960	5/1966	877,107
21C160	25 Squadron	4/1947	9/1948	11/1960	7/1967	934,417
21C161	73 Squadron	4/1947	1/1949		8/1964	701,443
21C162	17 Squadron	5/1947	1/1949	3/1959	7/1964	836,576
21C163	229 Squadron	5/1947	1/1949		8/1965	736,984

No	Name	Built	Renumbered	Rebuilt	Withdrawn	Final Mileages*
21C164	Fighter Command	7/1947	6/1948		5/1966	759,666
21C165	Hurricane	7/1947	6/1948		4/1964	730,489
21C166	Spitfire	9/1947	2/1949		9/1966	652,908
21C167	Tangmere	9/1947	7/1949		11/1963	688,269
21C168	Kenley	10/1947	9/1948		12/1963	700,417
21C169	Hawkinge	10/1947	6/1948		11/1963	673,643
21C170	Manston	11/1947	3/1949		8/1964	702,614
34071	601 Squadron	4/1948		5/1960	4/1967	782,028
34072	257 Squadron	4/1948			10/1964	698,843
34073	249 Squadron	5/1948			6/1964	684,325
34074	46 Squadron	5/1948			6/1963	639,592
34075	264 Squadron	6/1948			4/1964	643,241
34076	41 Squadron	6/1948			1/1966	803,425
34077	603 Squadron	7/1948		7/1960	3/1967	745,642
34078	222 Squadron	7/1948			9/1964	779,643
34079	141 Squadron	7/1948			2/1966	765,302
34080	74 Squadron	8/1948			9/1964	749,863
34081	92 Squadron	9/1948			8/1964	741,511
34082	615 Squadron	9/1948		4/1960	4/1966	697,386
34083	605 Squadron	10/1948			7/1964	737,467
34084	253 Squadron	11/1948			10/1965	663,249
34085	501 Squadron	11/1948		6/1960	9/1965	661,415
34086	219 Squadron	12/1948			6/1966	700,982
34087	145 Squadron	12/1948		12/1960	7/1967	704,638
34088	213 Squadron	12/1948		4/1960	3/1967	656,583
34089	602 Squadron	12/1948		11/1960	7/1967	661,252
34090	Sir Eustace Missenden Southern Railway	2/1949		8/1960	7/1967	743,948
34091	Weymouth	9/1949			9/1964	469,073
34092	City of Wells	9/1949			11/1964	502,864
34093	Saunton	10/1949		5/1960	7/1967	888,004
34094	Mortehoe	10/1949			8/1964	672,346
34095	Brentor	10/1949		1/1961	7/1967	796,614
34096	Trevone	11/1949		4/1961	9/1964	722,326
34097	Holsworthy	11/1949		3/1961	4/1966	743,659
34098	Templecombe	12/1949		2/1961	6/1967	819,105
34099	Lynmouth	12/1949			11/1964	628,771
34100	Appledore	12/1949		9/1960	7/1967	712,916
34101	Hartland	2/1950		9/1960	7/1966	568,479
34102	Lapford	3/1950			7/1967	593,438
34103	Calstock	2/1950			9/1965	629,172
34104	Bere Alston	4/1950		5/1961	6/1967	678,853
34105	Swanage	3/1950			10/1964	623,405
34106	Lydford	3/1950			9/1964	691,443
34107	Blandford Forum	4/1950			9/1964	665,130
34108	Wincanton	4/1950		5/1961	6/1967	808,361
34109	Sir Trafford Leigh-Mallory	5/1950		3/1961	9/1964	719,818
34110	66 Squadron	1/1951			11/1963	609,147

Note: Nos 21C101-21C170 renumbered by British Railways 34001-70 respectively.

With the exception of Nos 34095/7/9 and 34101/2/4, which were Eastleigh products, all the light Pacifics were built at Brighton Works. The following locomotives underwent a change of name during their working life:

No 34023	Blackmoor Vale to Blackmore Vale	April 1950
No 21C125	Rough Tor to Whimple	May 1948
No 34071	615 Squadron to 601 Squadron	August 1948
No 34092	Wells to City of Wells	March 1950
No 34107	Blandford to Blandford Forum	October 1952

*It should be noted that the official recording of mileages for the Bulleid Pacifics ceased late in 1964, after which records were kept by the motive power depots. It is probable that those engines which remained in traffic until 1967 ran a somewhat higher mileage than indicated.

Appendix Three

PRESERVED BULLEID PACIFICS

The Barry phenomenon has ensured that the Pacifics are very well represented in preservation, with no fewer than 11 members of the 'Merchant Navy' class and 20 light Pacifics still extant, though by no means all in working order. Several of the working examples have recently developed peripatetic tendencies. The locomotives' normal location is given below:

Loco No	Based at
34007	Plym Valley Railway
34010	Cargo Fleet, Teesside
34016*	Mid-Hants Railway
34023*	Bluebell Railway
34027*†	Severn Valley Railway
34028	Ashford Railway Trust
34039	Great Central Railway
34046	Brighton Works
34051	National Railway Museum York
34053	Severn Valley Railway
34058	Avon Valley Railway
34059	Bluebell Railway
34067	Mid-Hants Railway
34070	Richborough Power Station
34072*†	East Lancs Railway
34073	Brighton Works
34081	Nene Valley Railway
34092*†	Keighley & Worth Valley Railway
34101	Great Central Railway
34105*	Mid-Hants Railway
35005*	Great Central Railway
35006	Gloucestershire Warwickshire Railway
35009	Brighton Works
35010	North Woolwich Museum
35011	Brighton Works
35018	Mid-Hants Railway
35022	Swanage Railway
35025	Great Central Railway
35027*	Bluebell Railway
35028*†	Southall
35029	National Railway Museum (sectioned exhibit)

*Restored to active service
†Approved for main line operation

Right:
Cabside plaque carried by No 34067. *NRM*

SELECT BIBLIOGRAPHY

Allen, C. J. and Townroe, S. C. *The Bulleid Pacifics* (Ian Allan Ltd, 1976).
Austin, S., *Great Preserved Locomotives: 'Merchant Navy' No 35028 Clan Line* (Ian Allan Ltd, 1986).
Bradley, D. L., *Locomotives of the Southern Railway, Part 2* (The Railway Correspondence and Travel Society, 1976).
Bulleid, H. A. V., *Bulleid of the Southern* (Ian Allan Ltd, 1977).
Bulleid, H. A. V., *Master Builders of Steam* (Ian Allan Ltd, 1963).

Creer, S. and Morrison, B., *The Power of the Bulleid Pacifics* (Oxford Publishing Company Ltd, 1983).
Day-Lewis, S., *Bulleid — Last Giant of Steam* (George Allen & Unwin Ltd, 1964).
Fairclough, T. and Wells, A., *Southern Steam Locomotive Survey — Bulleid 'Merchant Navy' Pacifics* (D. Bradford Barton Ltd, 1976).
Fry, A. J., *Bulleid Power — the 'Merchant Navy' Class* (Alan Sutton Publishing Ltd., 1990).

Haresnape, B., *Bulleid Locomotives — A Pictorial History* (Ian Allan Ltd, 1977).
Nock, O. S., *Southern Steam* (David & Charles Ltd, 1966).
Robertson, K., *'Leader' and Southern Experimental Steam* (Alan Sutton Publishing Ltd, 1990).
Rogers, H. C. B., *Bulleid Pacifics at Work* (Ian Allan Ltd, 1980).
Winkworth, D. W., *Bulleid's Pacifics* (George Allen & Unwin Ltd, 1974).